## Praise for *A Pathway to Peace*

Every breast cancer survivor's story is also a story of co-survivors— of family and friends who are thrust into a new reality. Ben DuMont's candid account of his journey after his wife's diagnosis poignantly recounts how their experience led them to help others. Readers will be touched by the power of Ben's story and the strength of his love for his family.

—JUDY SALERNO, MD, MS
PRESIDENT & CEO, SUSAN G. KOMEN

*A Pathway to Peace* is engaging, extremely well written, and very edifying. I was quite moved by Ben's story, his faith, and the support both he and his wife gave and received throughout her cancer. It was a pleasure to read and will be helpful for others faced with a similar difficulty or any challenge.

—REV. DAN LAHART, SJ
PRESIDENT, STRAKE JESUIT COLLEGE PREPARATORY

Cancer is an incredibly personal experience for both the patient and the caregiver. By pouring his heart and emotions into *A Pathway to Peace*, Ben DuMont opens the door to a very private chapter of his and his wife Bridget's lives, allowing readers to join them on their moving journey.

—JODI WAYMOTH
MOTHER, BREAST CANCER SURVIVOR

Ben DuMont inspires readers by capturing the complexity of the human spirit in *A Pathway to Peace*. His writing elicits both the depths of fear and anguish as well as the heights of hope and faith in supporting his wife Bridget through her cancer. It is a gripping, uplifting story of raw emotion and a reminder of our God-given goodness, especially in harrowing times.

—DAVID LAUGHLIN
PRESIDENT, ST. LOUIS UNIVERSITY HIGH SCHOOL

# A Pathway to Peace

The Journey of a Cancer Co-Survivor

Ben DuMont

Dedicated to Bridget, Jack, and Andrew

# THE SERENITY PRAYER

God grant me the serenity
to accept the things I cannot change;
the courage to change the things I can;
and the wisdom to know the difference.

Living one day at a time;
Enjoying one moment at a time;
Accepting hardship as **a pathway to peace**;
Taking, as Jesus did, this sinful world
as it is, not as I would have it;
Trusting that You will make all things right
if I surrender to Your will;

So that I may be reasonably happy in this life
and supremely happy with You
Forever in the next.

*Amen.*

# CONTENTS

## ~ Part Three ~

## ~ Part Four ~

## ~ Epilogue ~

# A Pathway to Peace

The Journey of a Cancer Co-Survivor

PROLOGUE

# BIG WAD OF CASH

*** 

I pulled into the parking lot of Green Guys Landscaping on an unseasonably warm, muggy spring day, then sat in the car for a moment and waited. The air conditioner in my old Mustang did not work. Sweat slowly dripped from my pores as I pulled nine hundred dollars in cash from my pocket. They were all twenty-dollar bills, all forty-five of them. I counted twice to make sure.

I unbuckled my seat belt and paused before getting out of the car.

Emotion overcame me as I recalled the last six years of my life. Listening to Christian rock on the radio, I thought about how much pain and difficulty we had endured yet how blessed we had been. Things were different now. Heck, I was listening to Christian music, which I had loathed until several years earlier when my wife became hooked on it. Somehow, Bridget had convinced me that it was cool—at least, I occasionally listened to it because I liked the message and spirit and lyrics, a constant reminder of God's grace in our lives. There seemed to be more positive energy in my life now, and

I was more open to and aware of His presence, which was everywhere.

Tears welled in my eyes as I listened to a song by Tenth Avenue North:

> This is where the healing begins, oh
> This is where the healing starts
> When you come to where you're broken within
> The light meets the dark
> The light meets the dark...

When the song ended, I took a deep breath, wiped my eyes, and opened the door. The entrance was nearby, but it seemed the distance of a football field.

Nobody was around when I entered. The office was cool and spacious and had a backyard waterfall display in the lobby, a steady stream of water gently trickling down the rocky incline and spilling several feet below into a small pool. The serene sound of the water did little to ease my nerves.

After a couple of minutes, a woman entered. "Can I help you?"

"I'm dropping off some money for Dan."

"I'm sorry, he's not here."

I pulled out the wad of cash. "Can you give this to him?"

"What is this for?" She spoke cautiously.

"I'm paying for lawn service for a couple of families."

There was silence. *Whoever paid for lawn service upfront, in cash no less?* I wondered. Maybe she thought I had lost a bet. In any case, I felt the need to tell her what the money was for, though I did not want to make a big deal of it.

"The two families are dealing with cancer," I said. "My wife and I just started a charity, and we're trying to help them out."

Her demeanor changed instantly. "Really?" she replied, smiling now with wide radiant eyes. After pausing, she continued, "Yes...let me get you a receipt."

The woman carefully counted all of the money, occasionally shaking her head in disbelief, then gave me a receipt.

"I'll make sure Dan gets this," she said, holding the money and still smiling.

"Thank you."

I seemed to float across the parking lot back to my car. At long last, all of the pain and heartache seemed to have been worth it. Everything had finally come full circle. We were paying it forward now. The first families would benefit from our new charity, Bridget's Brigade, and feel some relief amid the stress, agony, and difficulty of cancer.

After Bridget's diagnosis, a few of my classmates from high school had arranged for a lawn service to help ease our burden. When they went to pay the company, the owner, who was a family friend, insisted on providing his service free of charge. Bridget and I always remembered Dan's kindness. He was just one of many family and friends who did more for us than we could have expected or imagined, and when we were able to help others through Bridget's Brigade, we called Dan. He was thrilled to help but would only allow us to pay him enough to cover his costs. Our discount, he said, could be used to help more families.

The healing had begun long ago, but this was the real healing, and it felt good. Like the song said, the light had, indeed, met the dark, and it shone brilliantly.

Driving home, I reflected on the book I was finishing. During and after Bridget's cancer treatment, I had written in a journal, and over time it developed into something more than a project intended simply to archive our past. Chapters and real-life characters developed, and my goal expanded to writing a book. It was difficult to find the time to write, however, and often it was all too easy to forget about our past. The intensity and emotion of our experience was too much. I would not write for ten months or more at a time. It was easier that way. After Bridget celebrated her five-year anniversary as a survivor, she asked when I planned to complete my book.

"I don't know," I said. "There's never any time to work on it."

"But you promised me you would finish it," she responded. "Do it for me. Do it for others who may benefit from it."

Now there were no more excuses, and no more motivation needed. Bridget had beaten cancer and only asked for one thing.

I always knew that I would be unable to fully capture our experience—punctuated by pain and suffering, and above all, the love and spirit of God and others—through mere words, but I would try. I would attempt to tell what happened from my own perspective, that of a young father fearful of an uncertain future yet moved to be fearless, to be a better person, to be more grateful, and most importantly, to believe. I would give it my best shot.

So here it goes. This is my story, if for nothing else, for Bridget.

# PART ONE

# THE RACE

### * * *

My heart pounded and my legs burned as I climbed the hill near the front of the pack. Sweat stung my eyes as I gasped for breath in the thick July air. I could smell the sweat in the main pack and feel the pain setting in the cyclists. Riders began to grimace, jostling for position and shouting at one another. "Watch it," one yelled, and another, "Keep your line!" Only three laps remained.

Bridget and Jack cheered from the crowd, and I waved back nonchalantly, hoping to intimidate the other riders. "What a day for a ride," I said out loud. Nobody responded. They were intensely focused. I was never big on mind games, but I was having fun.

We caught a momentary break on a slight descent. Dozens of bikes hummed in awesome unison, blazing violently downward and turning gently before beginning the ascent that would gradually plateau and bring us in agonizing formation, again, to the start/finish line.

The circuit was a one-mile loop through Carondelet Park, a historic landmark in the City of St. Louis dotted with picturesque lakes, hulking oaks, and rolling hills. Every Tuesday night during the summer, the course was blocked from traffic, allowing swarms of cyclists to let loose in a series of races sponsored by a local bike shop. I had raced the circuit several times, placing as high as second, third, and fourth, though victory still eluded me. In past races, I had never felt better or more in control than I now did. My cousin, an accomplished cyclist, had told me that when I was in top form I would feel as if I was riding on a motorcycle, and my body would respond like an engine. Jonny's prediction was now playing out. My legs, lungs, and heart tolerated and even thrived on the sudden accelerations, the attacks up the hill, and the constant intensity of the race. At times, it was as if I were playing a video game, focused on maintaining a top-ten position with minimal effort.

With two laps left, a teammate approached from behind. Chris was an older rider, short with muscular legs.

"Go ahead, Ben," he said.

It was his way of saying, "Let's work together to improve our odds of winning." But I took it as, "This is your chance, Ben. Make your break now."

Strategically, I had committed myself to conserving my energy until the last lap. This had been the linchpin to Jonny's success as a cyclist. I knew I would win if I had the discipline to sprint at the end, but no sooner. However, my confidence, adrenaline, and instinct, coupled with a voracious will to win, took over.

I glanced back at Chris, then at the rest of the pack. Nobody was making a break, and I grew restless. We were nearing the descent. It seemed like an ideal spot to make a break. I was fearless on descents and usually took more risks than others.

"Thanks," I said to Chris quietly, so as not to catch the attention of the other racers. I casually put my hands in the drops and switched into a higher gear, hoping the others would not notice me preparing for an attack. Then I took one last deep breath.

Without warning, I jumped out of my seat and exploded, stomping on my pedals, quickly passing the few cyclists ahead of me. The wind belted my body as I emerged from the draft of the pack, and in seconds I gained considerable speed and ground, screaming down the hill and leaning around the bend, my pedal nearly scraping the pavement at forty miles per hour. My momentum helped to carry me up the ascent. As I reached level ground near the start/finish line, the bell clanged for the final lap. The crowd was cheering.

"Go, Ben!" Bridget shouted. "You've got it!"

"Go Daddy, go!" yelled Jack.

I looked back for the first time and noticed I had made a successful breakaway. The pack was about fifty meters behind, though it seemed to be at my heels and losing patience. The bikes of more than sixty cyclists were grinding and gnashing loudly as the racers changed their gears.

On the final descent, I gave my legs a short rest, but I felt myself slipping. My heart had redlined, and I was gasping uncontrollably for breath. Lactic acid had accumulated in my legs like quick-drying cement, reducing them to heavy, burning mush stiffening by the second. With just a couple hundred meters left, I had hit the wall. No matter how hard I pedaled and tried to push through the pain, I could not. The pack was reeling me in at a relentless pace.

Within seconds, sixty hungry competitors had caught and pounced on their prey. The first few riders whizzed past and then, without warning, I was thrown from my bike. I had only fallen off my bike once since I began racing, when I took a downhill turn too fast and hit a pebble and slid on my side for twenty yards. Never had I been separated from my bike in a race. Everything seemed to occur in slow motion as I somersaulted forward, landing on my head and shoulder. Dazed and lying on the concrete, I quickly regained my senses and attempted to dodge passing riders. Another cyclist had fallen in front of me. He had clipped my handlebars and sent me sailing. After the pack passed, he helped me up.

"Sorry, man, I must've accidentally—"

I interrupted him. "It's part of racing."

He must have expected me to come up swinging, but I was more upset with myself. I had strayed from my strategy of conserving my energy until the final lap. I had been too headstrong and lacked discipline. It was my race to lose, and I had lost. I wanted to hit myself, but I could not move my right shoulder. Gently pressing my hand against my collarbone, I felt a lump.

With the aid of the cyclist, who was clad in a blindingly yellow jersey, I picked up my bike and limped off the pavement. He continued to apologize as a crowd quickly developed and surrounded us. Dizzy, I lay on the grass. My helmet was cracked, my arms and legs were bloodied, my uniform torn, and my right collarbone protruded like a golf ball underneath my jersey. Thankfully, the bone had not penetrated the skin.

A spectator created a makeshift sling for my shoulder by tying two rags together. Another asked if I needed an ambulance.

"I'm fine," I said. When I stood, I became somewhat faint. "Out of the way, I have to finish," I burst out, lunging for my bike.

"No!" everybody blurted in unison.

I paused, then smiled and chuckled. "Just kidding."

It was my way of trying to be Ernest Hemingway's archetypal hero exuding grace under pressure, but it came off as a failed attempt at comedy. I would never be a comedian—nor a professional cyclist.

# VISIONS

* * *

A trip to the emergency room confirmed that I had broken my right collarbone in four places and suffered a concussion. The pain in my collarbone was sharp and piercing, as if a dozen hornets were simultaneously stinging me. After a couple of days, the painkillers became nauseating. Driving my car to work proved a tricky feat, as I had to shift the gears with my left hand while trying to steer with it at the same time, my right arm limp and tender in a sling. Perhaps most frustrating, and progressively painful, a rub rash developed in my armpit because I could not move my shoulder or arm. It became infected and nearly impossible to clean, leaving an awful stench, and it was followed by a staph infection and regimen of antibiotics.

At home I was useless, coping with the pain and post-concussion symptoms. Jack constantly checked on me to make sure I was okay. He was only three, but already he had inherited his mother's habit of worrying. Though he was concerned, he thought my sling was pretty cool and wanted one of his own, so Bridget created one out of a T-shirt, and for days Jack walked around the house with his own arm immobilized.

My condition left Bridget to take care of everything—the house, the boys, and me. She had accumulated the responsibilities of a single parent overnight. If anybody could do it, though, it was Bridget. She was energetic and nurturing. The desire—and need—to help others was deeply ingrained in her.

As the days passed after my biking accident, I began to feel bad for Bridget. The added burden of taking care of me began to take a toll on her. Her acid reflux, which played havoc on her system particularly during stressful times, began to flare up. She made several visits to the doctor and underwent testing for her stomach. The medicine she received alleviated her symptoms only slightly.

Periodically, I began to think about what I would do without Bridget if something were to happen to her. What if some accident akin to mine were to happen to her? Or worse, what would happen if something far worse befell her and affected all of our lives? How would we cope? She was my soul mate, my confidante, and now my caretaker. How could we survive for even a day without her? I struggled with this notion.

At first, it seemed natural to have these thoughts. Bridget and I had a solid relationship, so I thought this anxiety was normal and signified my undying, unconditional love for her. However, several weeks after the accident, when my condition had improved and my collarbone had healed, these thoughts continued. In fact, they intensified and occurred more often, transforming from passing notions to compelling visions that arose on a regular basis. I would typically have these thoughts, or visions, while driving to and from work. During my forty-minute commute, I would envision the boys and me doing everything together without Bridget. I would be taking care of Jack and Andrew, doing all of the housework, going to the grocery store, reading to them at night, taking them where they needed to go, and being with them all of the time. Bridget was nowhere to be found, and I was Mr. Mom. While these visions were not always clear, well-defined, or in focus, their consistency convinced me that something would happen to Bridget, and that I was destined to take care of the boys on my own.

Initially, I was tormented with feelings of frustration, emptiness, and sadness, but as the weeks merged into months, a powerful yet unexplainable sense of comfort blanketed my being. The thoughts that had once pestered my mind now became frequent visions that enveloped my soul with peace. There was no single instance that symbolized this shift. Rather, it was a gradual, imperceptible transformation in the way I thought and felt. I became consummately fearless, imbued with infinite peace. I sensed that something terribly wrong would occur, but somehow everything would be fine.

I could not fathom how the fear and trepidation had slipped away. Had I lost grip on the reality, the enormity of possibly losing Bridget, be it temporarily due to an illness or accident, or—heaven forbid—if she were to die? Or had some higher power come upon me and bestowed gifts of grace, peace, and fortitude? Whatever the case, tragedy seemed imminent, but I felt strangely, overwhelmingly strong, confident, and at peace.

# HENRIETTA THE HEN

\* \* \*

B ridget and I had met at a bar, of all places. Just two years out of college, I had been traveling the country on an event-marketing gig for a top national bread-maker. During a brief visit home, I met some friends at a bar near Union Station in downtown St. Louis. It was a captivating setting, with a sprawling patio overlooking the cityscape capped by the Gateway Arch, its graceful silver sides shimmering brilliantly in the colorful downtown lights. A large crowd was on hand for a popular Eighties cover band playing outside. We enjoyed the tunes and lively conversation in the crisp early autumn air, catching up on the past several months I had been away.

During intermission, I spotted one of my sister's friends, Jen. My sister Megan had wanted to set me up with her, though I thought of Jen as more of an extended family member than a girlfriend. As she approached, I felt in somewhat of a bind. Jen was with an attractive friend with short, stylish blond hair, big blue eyes, and a gleaming smile.

After we exchanged greetings, Jen introduced us. "This is Bridget," she said.

Bridget was more than just a cute blonde. She exuded class, beamed with positive energy, and spoke with confidence and sincerity.

I went out of my way to shake her hand. Ordinarily, I would not have done so, feigning disinterest and playing my part in the cat-and-mouse dating game. However, something was different. I felt palpably, irresistibly magnetized to Bridget.

We invited the girls to watch the band with us, and as we walked back to our table, I stayed next to Bridget so that I could sit by her. As the night progressed, I became more intrigued by her. Every time she spoke, my heart fluttered. The feeling was indescribable, something I had never experienced. I did not want the night to end, nor did I want to leave her side. Giddy and nervous with excitement, I reached over and held Bridget's hand beneath the table. We looked at each other and giggled childishly. The others did not know what to make of us. "What are you two laughing at?" they asked. At the time, I even envisioned being married to Bridget, but I did not think I would be that lucky.

My determination to pursue Bridget trumped any ounce of charm I may have had when it was time to leave. After the others had gone and we were left standing alone, I gave her a kiss, then casually handed her my business card and told her to call me the next day.

She laughed. "I don't call guys," she said, and politely gave me her phone number. "You call me."

I knew I only had one chance with Bridget, as I was leaving town soon. If I didn't pursue her, somebody else would. Instead of waiting to call her, I nervously phoned early the following afternoon and we made plans to meet that night with some friends at a bar. As my friends and I waited for them to show, we had our doubts. It was more than an hour after we had planned to meet, and they still were not there. My heart sank, and I wondered if I should have waited longer to call her. When Bridget and her friends finally walked in, my spirits lifted and I knew that I still had a chance. We talked all night. I learned that we shared a common faith and had both attended Catholic schools growing up. Bridget had a brother, Sean, who was my age. Unbeknownst to us, we had played baseball against one another in grade school. Bridget and I laughed when we realized that we had probably seen each other long ago at the games. We had several mutual friends and traded stories about them. I was attracted to her positive, magnetic energy, her humor, and her radiant, innocent smile. I felt at ease when I was with her, like nothing else mattered but the mere fact that I was with her.

We went out again the following night to see a movie before I hit the road for a few months. I quickly felt homesick when I was away from Bridget, the same empty feeling I had experienced as a kid going to camp and leaving my family for the first time.

The road began wearing on me, and I finally seemed open to pursuing security and stability, notions from which I had been running since childhood. In high school and college, I had taken great pride in living for the moment. I was spontaneous, adventurous, independent, and at times rebellious. At age fifteen, I studied abroad in Sydney, Australia, for six months because I wanted to see the world and experience another culture firsthand. I spent seven entire summers during my adolescence on a remote Canadian island as part of a wilderness adventure camp, leading grueling canoe trips across the vast network of northern lakes. One summer in college, I worked on a dude ranch in Colorado exploring the sprawling, awe-inspiring Continental Divide. Much of my life I had made a livelihood—literally and figuratively—seeking fun and adventure and new experiences. It was my mission to go further, do more, and laugh all the while. New thrills loomed beyond the blue horizon, and I raced feverishly to catch them. I had always viewed life experiences as an investor values money—the more

I had, the better off I would be. I thought I had made some good investments consistent with my belief that memories, not money, endure and provide lasting value. But all of the restless activity had left me empty. Something, or somebody, seemed to be missing. The uncertainty of my future needed clarity and meaning. Lonely, I longed for somebody to fill the void.

After meeting Bridget, my life finally began to take on new and added value. Being away from each other while I was working on the road strengthened our relationship because it allowed us to get to know one another without distractions, and it made us appreciate our time together. We would talk on the phone for hours and instant-message one another over the Internet. I always looked forward to hearing "You've got mail" from AOL and reading a note from Bridget. At times we would be chatting online, as I was heading to bed after a late night in some distant city while she was getting ready to go to work. Separated by hundreds of miles and multiple time zones, we shared a bond, a closeness that felt like we were together. Bridget quickly became a stabilizing force in my life, providing direction and, above all, companionship.

Near the end of my tour on the road, I bought Bridget a plane ticket to California and planned a week-long trip along the coast. From Los Angeles, we visited Santa Barbara and traveled north to Morro Bay near San Luis Obispo, referred to by the locals as "SLO." I had heard that the pace was, indeed, rather slow in SLO. "The police will give you a ticket for going five miles an hour under the speed limit," a co-worker once said, but everybody agreed that San Luis Obispo was one of the greatest destinations in California. Nestled about ten miles inland on the central coast, SLO was bathed in natural beauty with vast views of rolling vineyard hills.

We visited a couple of wineries near SLO on Valentine's Day. It was a weekday, so there were few others around. En route to a winery in the early afternoon, we climbed a long incline to a pristine lake surrounded by lush verdant hills that protruded gently into the sky. We were among puffy low-hanging clouds and enjoyed a spectacular vantage of the vistas. I pulled off the road near the lake, and we sat at the edge of the water and soaked in the stillness of the surroundings. It was quiet and peaceful in the heart of wine country.

I leaned toward Bridget and embraced her. "I love you," I said. She smiled, held me tightly, and did not let go.

That evening, after we enjoyed a late Italian dinner and strolled the beach under the moonlight, I prayed. Since adolescence, I had made a nightly ritual of talking to God, and on this night I said a special prayer in thanksgiving for Bridget. As the tide soothingly slapped the beach, the stunning array of stars shone down on a lively gang of pelicans nearby, and I thought about our future together. Bridget had been the missing link in my life, and after we met I knew I could not lose her, ever.

When we first met, Bridget was a geography teacher at a public middle school. Lively, effervescent, and naturally attractive, she must have been the chatter of the hormone-budding boys in her class. She earned the "Teacher of the Year Award," a significant achievement considering there were a hundred other teachers in her school. Bridget was most proud of always trying to help the underprivileged and unpopular students, the ones shunned by their peers. Thoughtfulness and a caring spirit embodied her character, especially on birthdays— holidays that, in her estimation, were second only to Christmas because they provided opportunities to do something special for others.

The leadership Bridget exuded as a teacher was a gift that she had developed at an earlier age. In junior high, she ran for president of student council against a heavily favored opponent. Bridget was committed and relentless with her campaign, spending hours on writing her speech and working late at night with friends to make posters, signs, and flyers. Her resolve paid off, and she won. When the decision was announced, her opponent's supporters were waiting with flowers because they assumed she would win. Bridget had ruined their victory party. She later said she enjoyed being the underdog. It challenged her to set bigger goals and coincided with her "go big or go home" philosophy.

While Bridget was widely known as the head of student council in junior high, she had a nickname privy to only a handful of close friends: Henrietta the Hen. Her brothers were eager to tell me all about it shortly after I met her. They said in high school Bridget worked part-time as a hostess at a pizza place that was popular for its arcade. Several of her friends worked there as well—the girls as hostesses and the guys as game room staffers. Parents frequently threw birthday parties for their children at the restaurant. Bridget would dress up as one of the restaurant's mascots, Henrietta the Hen, and parade around with the kids, dancing to music in her purple tights and webbed feet and goofy white hen costume capped with a big red pointy top. Such was the scourge of being a tall girl with lanky legs, and thus, the one best suited for the costume. One night, after all of the guests had left, several of her co-workers kidnapped Henrietta and put her in a shopping cart from the store next door and pushed her around the parking lot laughing and goofing and singing, the big hen immobile in the cart and giggling with a broad beaked smile. Thankfully no eggs were hatched in the process.

I quickly fell in love with Bridget—her hen past aside—simply because she was filled with love herself. She had integrity and character, and she put me at ease whether we were alone or with others. In her presence, I never felt any social anxiety or awkwardness that I may have had. She was far more outgoing and extroverted than I and once admitted that she could talk to a wall if she had to. I felt so comfortable around her that she seemed like a best friend, as opposed to a cute blonde I was courting.

Once, after I took her for a date to a winery in a scenic rural area west of St. Louis, I drove a different route home, one that took us further away.

"Where are we going?" she asked.

"Just wait, it's a surprise."

I had the urge to make a blazing fire and sleep under the stars, even though Bridget had never been camping and we were both dressed in nice clothes. I kept my camping gear in my trunk and knew of a campground nearby. When we arrived at Robertsville State Park, I laughed and said, "Here we are."

"Where is this? What are we doing?"

"We're at the Ritz. Now let's get some firewood."

Instead of demanding that I take her home, she went along with it and helped gather kindling in her skirt and high heels, nearly twisting an ankle as she combed the woods.

The park ranger drove by and asked, "What are you all doing?" He looked bewildered when I said we were camping.

Once we had collected enough wood, I constructed a teepee made of twigs and small branches with bark inside, giving Bridget the play-by-play as I placed each stick methodically and carefully like an acupuncturist inserting needles into a patient's skin. "Remember, when making a fire, always pretend you only have one match," I said.

She laughed and seemed mildly impressed that I was able to make a fire successfully with a single match. It was her first campfire, her first experience sleeping in the woods, and, somehow, she had enjoyed it. In fact, she wanted to go again, and we did frequently in the future. I knew it was true love when not only had she not jumped out of the car on the way to the park, but also when her friends asked me in disbelief, "You took Bridget camping?" My affirmative response was quickly followed with an astonished "Seriously?"

After Bridget and I dated for a couple of years, we married and had two boys. She quit her teaching job to stay home and care for Jack after he was born, and then two years later we had Andrew. In addition to starting a sewing and embroidery business that she ran from home, she continued working part-time as a tutor for a program that served out-of-school students. Bridget worked long hours and enjoyed being a mother above all else. She joined a preschool mothers group to meet new friends and would host play dates at our house. Caring for Jack and Andrew was a blessing that she valued and cherished.

Family had always been important to Bridget, and she knew of both its goodness as well as its fragility. She was very close with her mom, but after her dad left the family when Bridget was in middle school, she became even more attached to Sandy, who was forced to go back to work full-time to help provide for four teenagers after sixteen years of being a stay-at-home mom. Sandy's kids spanned just five years. Shannon was the oldest, then Sean, followed by Bridget and her younger brother Brian. Bridget learned from her mom the values of sacrifice and doing good deeds for others. Sandy worked hard so her children could have what they needed, and at times what they wanted. This allowed the boys, avid athletes, to play multiple sports and the family to take trips and the girls to continue their lifestyles. The kids, in turn, pitched in to do their part, with Sean and Brian working as caddies and at car washes, Shannon working her way up as a manager at a restaurant, and Bridget dressing up as Henrietta the Hen at the arcade-pizza joint. Sandy lived by a simple motto: "However you handle things is how your kids will handle them." She took it to heart after her divorce by making the best of a bad situation so her kids would be affected as little as possible. Bridget always remembered this advice.

The connectedness of Bridget's family, despite her parents' divorce, was deeply ingrained and started at an early age. Sandy had a twin sister, Suzy, who lived nearby. Suzy had three sons whom Bridget regarded as brothers. When she was little, she wanted to keep up with the boys. After much pleading, her brothers and cousins would let her "play" baseball with them. They would tell her to climb the backyard fence and give her a glove to catch foul balls, convincing her it was a real position. Bridget was excited to be included and would scale the chain link fence in her dress and towhead pigtails with matching ribbons. The two families lived only five doors apart and went on summer vacations together. Bridget's Uncle Dan—Suzy's husband—drove her and the other kids to middle school everyday. After high school, Bridget went to the University of Kansas, while her brothers and cousins all attended the Jayhawks' archrival, the University of Missouri. She would go back and forth with them, trading jabs about the football and basketball teams. It was always a lopsided argument, as Bridget was far outnumbered, but the two parties enjoyed the ribbing regardless of who was on the winning side. "The boys" loved their sister and cousin and were protective of her in a fraternal way.

The first time I went to Bridget's house to meet her mom and stepdad, I was running a little late. It boded well for me. After I met Sandy and Dave, Bridget and I set off to see a movie and she told me what I had missed.

"All the boys were at our house waiting to meet you," she said, referring to her brothers and cousins. "You took too long to get here so they left."

While waiting for me to arrive, they had plotted various ways to "meet" me like changing into old raggedy clothing to embarrass Bridget and rearranging her mom's decorative letter blocks to read "We love you, Benny."

"They said they couldn't believe I'm going out with a guy who drives a purple truck and wears cowboy boots," Bridget said. "I didn't go on a second date with a guy once for wearing black tennis shoes with white socks, so they had to see you for themselves."

It was true. I was driving an eighteen-wheeler painted with bright purple and multi-colored animated characters as part of my event-marketing job. Our chase vehicle was a van painted in the same scheme, one impossible to miss. When we were back home on break we would drive the purple van, and so on our date night I did pick up Bridget in the "purple beast," as I referred to it, and I wore cowboy boots.

"I planned that one right," I said.

After the movie, we met up with her brothers and cousins for a drink and laughed about their antics and scheming.

Following our wedding, Bridget and I moved in to a house near Sandy and Dave on the west side of St. Louis. I had wanted to live closer to the city, but the homes in the county had more room and were more affordable. Moreover, Bridget and I knew that when we had kids, living close to Sandy and Dave would be to everybody's benefit. All of Bridget's brothers and cousins and her sister also moved nearby. As in the past, the two families that had grown up just five doors apart now lived within five miles of one another and met regularly for birthdays and holidays and the simple occasion of throwing a party at Sandy and Dave's, events marked by a lively atmosphere and towering bonfires.

"Lucky you, Benny," her brothers and cousins would joke. "Little did you know that when you married Bridget, you married her whole family."

# FABULOUS YELLOW
# ROMAN CANDLES

* * *

The man in the elevator had a serene presence about him. He was an African American with a goatee, dressed modestly in a baggy T-shirt, khaki work pants, and tennis shoes. He wore a gold necklace tucked beneath his shirt. In his hand he clutched a book.

"Accident?" he asked, referring to my sling.

"Biking accident," I replied. "Broken collarbone."

He glanced at me and grinned, his eyes gleaming. I had seen him before. In fact, we frequently passed each other in the hallways and said hello, though I didn't know his name, nor how long he had been working at the school. I only knew he was a janitor. He must have only been here a few months— it was as though he just began appearing quietly and unannounced. I had intended to introduce myself at some point, but the moment never presented itself. Perhaps we did not need a formal introduction.

"You ever read about St. Ignatius?" he asked in his wispy voice, referring to the book in his hand.

I had some background on Ignatius, as I had attended a Jesuit high school—the same school, in fact, at which I now worked. I was in my fourth year on staff in the school's development office. St. Ignatius of Loyola founded the Society of Jesus, commonly known as the Jesuits, in 1540. Since then, the Jesuits had responded to human needs in a variety of ministries throughout the world, with a particular focus in education. In addition to St. Ignatius' incredible leadership and vision, his most notable characteristic was his ability to find God in all things. After more than 450 years since their founding, the Jesuits, affectionately referred to as the "Jebbies," had thrived as the largest Catholic order in the world.

Just as the Jesuits had endured through the ages, so had they remained a constant in my life. As a teenager, I had the opportunity to attend two Jesuit high schools, one in my hometown and another in Australia for a semester. Now, years after graduation, I had returned to work at my alma mater. I enjoyed the experience of working with and learning from the few Jesuits that remained. The Jesuits were highly intellectual but also unpretentious, a combination that made for ideal mentors and conversationalists. Above all, as their name suggested, Jesuits strived to actively live in the model of Jesus Christ. They did more than merely preach from pulpits. They were contemplatives in action, "men for others" who believed in helping souls through their good works.

From a young age, I had been exposed to the richness of the Jesuit tradition. Aside from my parents, it was the Jebbies—and one in particular, Father Paul—to whom I was most indebted for providing me the tools for success in life, a life full of spiritual meaning, value, and significance.

In the late 1970s, Father Paul founded a not-for-profit organization that gave futures to underprivileged boys. It later evolved to help girls as well and expanded internationally to transform the lives of at-risk kids by providing them with stable homes, strong educations, and financial and emotional support. Shortly after the program's founding, Father Paul started a wilderness adventure camp in Ontario, Canada, where he brought together boys from broken homes, otherwise known as "program" kids, with peers from more stable upbringings. This unique blend of backgrounds was the basis, or magic, of the camp. In addition to Father Paul, other Jesuits were involved with the camp as counselors and camp directors. Their leadership and example were vital in the spiritual development of both campers and staff members alike.

My brother Matt, a few years older than I, attended the camp just before entering high school, and shortly thereafter Father Paul recruited my mom to help cook. We all attended the camp together, my mom as the head cook, my brother as a staffer, and I as a camper. My younger sister Megan even joined my mom some summers when she was not attending another camp in Minnesota. After a couple of summers, I became a staff member as well, doing maintenance work and leading canoe trips and teaching classes such as canoeing and fishing and sailing.

Given the amount of time I spent at the camp—about two months every summer for seven years—the Jesuits became integral in my development as a young man. Not only did they instill confidence in me through challenging activities such as canoeing, hiking, and wilderness survival trips, they reinforced the power of prayer and promoted a world view that emphasized justice and service beyond the periphery of my own life. I befriended kids whose parents were drug addicts or in prison, if they had parents at all. I learned to not take things for granted. Jesus Christ was a real part of my life, I realized, and if I had an open mind, I, too, like St. Ignatius, could see God in all things.

"He was incredible, incredible," the man in the elevator now said of St. Ignatius. He was holding up his book as he referred to it. I did not see the title of the book, as I was focused on his eyes. "It's good stuff, good stuff. Powerful, powerful."

The man's genuine enthusiasm for St. Ignatius was impressive, even moving.

When the elevator opened, he said, "All right now" and exited. It was his way of saying goodbye.

As I continued ascending, I was overcome with a strange, spontaneous sense of emotion. It was refreshing, powerful, pure, and above all, joyful. I wanted to burst out laughing. I felt as if I were in the presence of a man who had inspired me as a teenager through his novels and philosophy on life—Jack Kerouac. The beatnik author had a voracious zeal for life and a longing for something far greater than himself, something divine. In his epic novel *On the Road*, Kerouac wrote, "The only people for me are the mad ones, the ones who are mad to live, mad to talk, mad to be saved...the ones who never yawn or say a commonplace thing, but burn, burn, burn like fabulous yellow roman candles exploding like spiders across the stars and in the middle you see the blue centerlight pop and everybody goes 'Awww!'" It was as though the man, whose name I later learned was Isaac, and I were kindred souls connecting through a brief, unexpected encounter.

In the following days, I would see Isaac more often, and he frequently carried his book on St. Ignatius. He was always courteous yet reserved. I learned that he was the brother of Dee, the school's head custodian. Everybody, including the students, knew and liked Dee, who had been working at the school for three decades. Friendly and gregarious, he wore a smile at all times. Isaac was as likeable as Dee, though more introverted.

Isaac was an ordinary man with an ordinary profession, but he seemed to have an extra-ordinary spirit. When he mopped floors and cleaned classrooms, he was deeply focused and acutely attentive. He was in harmony with his work, and the look in his eyes suggested he was also in harmony with the Holy Spirit. Perhaps he had learned from reading about Ignatius to relish and experience God in the monotony and routine of everyday. Either way, it was refreshing to see a man with such inner peace, particularly in an age where dollars had replaced dreams and image verged on eradicating character. It had become apparent to me that, although we had never had a lengthy conversation, the Holy Spirit beamed quietly from his being.

When my collarbone healed, I began training in earnest for the time trial state championship. I bought a set of rollers, a simple yet ingenious piece of training equipment that actually requires balance and agility, unlike a standard indoor cycling trainer. The rollers were ideal for maintaining proper form throughout the off-season. I was also riding with my team, which was sponsored by a local bike shop, during the winter, several times in the snow. My form, endurance, and strength gained momentum in tandem with my experience and confidence.

Things finally seemed to be settling down. We had faced a set of challenges that year: the stressful, time-consuming process of moving; a visit to the emergency room to stitch Jack up after a fall; another hospital visit with Andrew to get tubes in his ears; and, finally, my biking accident. By the end of the year, the physical and mental stresses in our lives were, at last, behind us, and we looked ahead with a breath of fresh air. Jack, three, and Andrew, one, were growing older and becoming more manageable. They now had a cul-de-sac in the front of our house where they could ride their bikes, as well as a fenced-in backyard where they played freely.

After the leaves fell and the quietude of winter was upon us, I would occasionally think about the mysteriously mesmerizing custodian at our school. At Christmas, I wondered what Isaac was doing, where he was going to Church, and whether he had a family. I did not know him well, but when I thought about him my soul lifted. I felt at peace and close to God, and like St. Ignatius, if but for a moment, I could divine our world as God's cathedral, and every second had the potential of being holy, transcendent, and everything a gift, an opportunity to experience His love and spirit in my life.

Isaac's quiet entrance into my life, oddly enough, coincided with the onset of the visions of Bridget's absence. Little did I know how real my visions would soon become—or how desperately I would need Isaac and all the other people through whom God worked in our lives.

# PART TWO

# NEED FOR SPEED

### * * *

Accelerating onto the highway, my Mustang revving and rumbling, I sped toward the city early on a Saturday evening. Marilyn Manson belted out his lyrical fisticuffs as the crisp spring air spilled into the car. It was an old Manson album titled *Holy Wood*, which my brother had given me years earlier. I was never much of a Manson fan and had only listened to the CD a few times, but the music was perfect for the moment, like caffeine for the psyche. I had recently listened to the album on a particularly rigorous workout on my rollers when I knocked out fifty miles in two hours. Just two weeks earlier, Manson helped me to prepare mentally before our team time trial. Our team had won the competition. I couldn't take much credit for the victory, but nonetheless, Manson had pumped up my body and mind for the event. When it was time for a fight, it was Manson time.

Now it was Manson time again.

Bridget had come down with strep throat and would be unable to go with me to my friend's wedding reception that night. She was getting ready to go to her mom and Dave's house with the boys and had just come out of the shower.

"I think I felt a lump," she said, garbed in her robe.

"What?" I had been putting on my tie and stopped in mid-motion.

"I think I felt a lump in my breast while I was in the shower." At first she sounded worried. Then her worry turned to panic, even terror. "I hope I don't have breast cancer."

"I'm sure it's nothing," I said. "There's probably some explanation for it. It's probably benign, whatever it is."

Bridget had always been a worrier, so it came as no surprise that she automatically envisioned the direst possibility. My lack of worrying usually helped to balance our relationship. I was an optimist who tried to keep things in perspective. It was easier to have a positive and realistic outlook now, given the fact that Bridget was young, only thirty, healthy, active, and had no family history of cancer.

"Look, honey, there are any number of things it could be," I said emphatically. Even as an optimist, I could not deny the gravity of the situation. "But just to be safe, call the doctor first thing Monday."

I felt somewhat guilty about leaving her with the boys. Jack and Andrew were unusually crabby, and Bridget's ailment had been amplified by this new anxiety.

I began to take on her mood as I drove to the reception. The visions had re-emerged and confronted me head on. No longer were they mere thoughts in the innermost lobe of my cerebrum. They had instantly, inexplicably transformed to tangible reality, and they rocked my core.

Preoccupied with my thoughts and absorbed in the music, I weaved gently through the light freeway traffic. I felt totally comfortable and in control when I was speeding. In a sense, I had been chasing speed for much of my life. In high school, I applied to the Air Force Academy to become a fighter pilot, but rescinded my application when, in the spirit of juvenile abandon, I decided I wanted to have fun in college. I still had ambitions to become a fighter pilot after college, but it was too late. I had never had the resources to become a race-car driver, but I believed that if I had the money I could match Michael Schumacher or Jeff Gordon. My passion for speed was displayed on the cake for our wedding rehearsal dinner. Several plastic, Matchbox-like cars were placed randomly around an oval race-track. Brightly colored iced lettering alluded to the "race of our lives." Aside from our honeymoon, that was my most significant contribution to our wedding planning. Now, years after our wedding, I was speeding down the freeway in a car I had purchased to help satisfy my hunger for speed.

I arrived early at the Missouri History Museum for the reception. Apparently I had been driving too fast. I waited outside to kill time and ease my nerves. The museum was situated in the heart of Forest Park, a crown jewel of the city that featured several popular civic attractions and hundreds of acres of lush, rolling greenery. Everybody contently went about their daily lives: joggers and cyclists traversed the pathways of the picturesque park in the gleam of the golden hour; and a family set up a picnic on a sprawling blanket of grass at the base of a towering oak, as ducks skidded onto a nearby pond rippling from the gentle wake of ornate fountains.

The fear of the unknown continued to prey on my mind. *Were the visions real? Could Bridget really have cancer? Was something awful going to happen to her?* All the while, the wave of comfort that had previously eased my spirit continued to lift me up. While I did not know what was going to happen, I somehow felt supremely confident and in control. If Bridget did have breast cancer, I would be ready. I was totally focused for the racing season, but I could transform that energy to a more intense fight if need be.

Gazing at the tranquil scene in the park, however, I thought it was all nonsense. Surely it was nothing, I thought. *The doctor will smile and say she's fine.*

# KIDDO

### * * *

B ridget could not get an appointment with her OBGYN on Monday, so she opted to see a nurse practitioner that afternoon. She told Bridget to get a mammogram at her leisure just to be safe, but she was not overly concerned. There seemed no reason to panic at the time, but Bridget still tried to get the test as soon as possible. The few hospitals she called were booked for several weeks, and she was too young to get tested at any of the mammogram vans. Bridget's friend Susie called a nearby hospital and was able to get an appointment for her on Thursday, the earliest available slot in town. She went to the mammogram alone because the nurse practitioner had not given her any indication to be worried.

As Bridget was getting her mammogram, I made last-minute preparations for our school's upcoming auction. The mood in our office and among the parent volunteers was tense. It was our biggest event of the year, the major fundraiser that generated significant funds to help keep tuition affordable and maintain the socio-economic diversity of our student body. Hundreds of volunteers, led by our office and the Mothers' Club, spearheaded the effort of raising more than a half million dollars annually through the auction.

The theme for this year's auction was "Under the Big Top," and the decorating crew had begun in earnest to transform the gymnasium two weeks earlier. Red and white drapery hung low from the ceiling, giving the impression of a gigantic circus tent. Popcorn machines were interspersed throughout, and a stuffed replica of a trapeze artist dangled from a swing high in the rafters. The perimeter of the gymnasium was lined with auction items spanning from furniture and jewelry to sports memorabilia and gift baskets.

I was amid the clutter and chaos, working with our tech staff to ensure the projectors were in place for the oral auction presentation, when my cell phone rang.

"Ben," Bridget blurted.

She rarely called me by my name, so when she said "Ben," I knew it was serious. Then she began crying.

"You have to come to the hospital," she said. "Get to the hospital. I need you."

I rushed to my car and sped to the hospital, listening to Marilyn Manson again at full tilt. My heart pounded and my stomach turned itself inside out as I weaved from lane to lane. Bridget's words demanding I get to the hospital reverberated chillingly in my mind.

When I arrived, Bridget was in the doctor's office with her mom, who had arrived moments earlier. Her eyes were already swollen from crying.

Things happened quickly. A nurse came in to say the doctor would arrive momentarily. I usually had good intuition about first impressions, and I sensed something was terribly wrong with the nurse's body language. She was timid and uncomfortable. We all knew if the results were negative, there would be no need to see the doctor. Bridget sobbed.

When the doctor entered, her crying intensified. We tried to console her. Without saying anything, the doctor put his hand on her shoulder, and at that moment, our darkest prospect, our greatest fear was confirmed.

The doctor looked like a young grandfather, with spectacles and a balding head. When he spoke, he exuded confidence and impeccable bedside manner. He affectionately referred to Bridget as "kiddo." It was apparent that, beyond his professionalism and doctor-speak, he felt connected and affected in some way, almost as if he were speaking to somebody he had known for years, or perhaps to his daughter's best friend. It had been his day off. He happened to be visiting the office for just a moment when a nurse told him about Bridget. He was in his street clothes and sacrificed an entire hour consulting with us, in addition to further time to perform a core biopsy procedure. We later learned he was the hospital's chief of surgery and director of the breast cancer center. He was Czech with a long last name that started with a K, so we would refer to him simply as Dr. K. It fit well, as K was also for "kiddo."

"I have to be honest, kiddo," he said. "It doesn't look good. I'm ninety-nine percent sure you have cancer, but we need to do further testing to see what we're dealing with."

There it was. My nagging visions seemed to be coming true, like a bad dream unfolding before my eyes. In less than a week, Bridget had detected a lump and received confirmation of the worst. We reeled at the dreadful news, hugging each other and crying. Dr. K could only speculate about Bridget's cancer but told us about the varying kinds and levels it could be and the numerous types of treatments that would likely include chemotherapy. The news was difficult to digest, the information too much to absorb. It was accentuated by frustration, even anger at the other hospitals that said they could not admit Bridget for a mammography for several weeks. *What if we had waited another several weeks for her to get tested?* I wondered.

The nurse said they would call us later in the afternoon with details regarding the cancer after evaluating the biopsy sample.

When we left, Bridget's stepdad Dave was waiting for us outside the doctor's office. Sandy had already called him with the news. He had earned the respect of Bridget and her family over the years with his solid character and unwavering loyalty to Sandy. Dave had a special bond with Jack and Andrew, who affectionately referred to him as "Pawpaw." He had even quit smoking, a habit he acquired as a teenager, because he did not want to set a bad example for Sandy's grandchildren. A shop teacher at a technical institute, Dave was the ultimate handyman, and we had benefited from his vast expertise on several home projects. He had once been a commander in the Navy, a fitting position for a man who was conservative, tough, disciplined, industrious and, in the best sense, old-school.

Dave met us in a windowed walkway that connected the building to the parking lot. He looked sullen, with his head down. When he saw Bridget he embraced her and began to cry openly. He tried to talk, but his words were indecipherable. Sandy later said she had never seen Dave cry. It was the first time I'd ever seen a grown man cry with such intensity, and it rattled me. Standing in the walkway totally exposed to the sun, I felt completely helpless, exposed, and naked to the future.

# OLD BUDDY

\* \* \*

W e had never read the manual on how to react after a cancer diagnosis—if such a text exists—so we did not know what to do or think on the ride home from the hospital. I had already made my one phone call to my mom as I drove the car and told her while sobbing that our worst fear had come true. I was not in the mood to talk to anybody else. She would tell the rest of our family. Now that word was out about her diagnosis, Bridget and I looked at each other, confused, angry, scared, and speechless. Questions swirled in our minds, with no answers. *Why did this happen to us? How could it happen? How would we confront cancer while juggling our roles at work and as parents? What if Bridget only had months to live? What would we tell Jack and Andrew, and how would they react?* The uncertainties were daunting and dizzying.

Eventually we decided to stop by the grocery store. It was the most normal thing we could have done at this moment when everything in our lives had instantly, unalterably, become abnormal. We needed food, and the boys were taken care of at her sister's house, so we had time.

I left Bridget in the car so she could talk to her dad in California. Dennis had moved to San Diego a few years earlier with Bridget's stepmom. While Bridget did not see her dad often, he would always be her father, and she felt compelled to call him.

As I walked through the store, I was hoping, somehow, that I would wake up from this nightmare. Everybody went about their normal routines, uninterrupted, fluid, and seemingly content. The sounds of the cash registers were louder than I had ever recalled, like a crowded arcade or casino. A woman passed by, casually talking on her cell phone about how she had just finished working out and was going to pick up the kids, her words amplified and echoing in my mind. It was as if some primordial survival instinct had taken over. I noticed every little visual and auditory detail. When the lady at checkout asked if I wanted paper or plastic, I wanted to shout out that I was more interested in whether my wife was going to live or die than the material of my grocery bag.

On my way back to the car, I heard somebody call my name. At first, I thought it was my imagination. I wished the whole day was just a bad dream, so I decided to ignore whoever it was, until the person called from behind again. As I turned around, I saw an old, familiar face.

"What's up, old buddy?" he said, smiling and walking toward me.

He was only a few feet from me. I had to talk, or try to.

I had not seen Todd in ten years since our internship at the ad agency where we met. It was our first real job after college. He had specialized in account service, while I was in the creative department. Todd and I were part of a group of six other interns. We were a tight-knit bunch and spent a lot of time together outside of work. I had always valued my friendship with Todd. He was a good conversationalist and it was good to see him, but I didn't think I could summon the strength for small-talk in my emotional state. The situation was already unbearable.

"Hey, Todd," I said. My body language was speaking volumes, I was well aware. "Not much going on. How are you?"

"Doing great. I'm just running an errand on a sales call," he said.

We walked out to the parking lot together and stood in front of the store, where we continued our painful conversation. I asked about his job, and he went on and on, but I was not listening. It was hard to even make eye contact. I didn't want him to think I was uninterested in seeing him, so I felt compelled to tell him about Bridget when he asked about me.

"Actually, things are not fine," I said. Tears filled my eyes. "I just found out my wife's got cancer."

I could not hold back. It was uncomfortable and embarrassing, considering our friendship had been based solely on social outings and good times with our intern clan. We had never endured any difficulty together, and certainly nothing like I was experiencing. Part of me felt bad for spilling my guts. If we were women, we might have been hugging and dabbing each other's eyes with tissues. Instead, we were left with the inevitable "guy" awkwardness.

Todd had left advertising to pursue sales in another industry. Coincidentally, he was now an account representative for a major genetics testing company focused specifically on breast cancer patients.

Todd began talking about the importance and intricacies of genetic testing, delving into the subjects of proteins and chromosomes and genes as if it were biology class. Before we parted he invited me to his car to give me some informational pamphlets. Todd's attempts to educate me were admirable, but I only learned how easy it was to become overwhelmed and inundated with information, particularly regarding a topic that baffled even the brightest doctors. Granted, my mind was so clouded I was not digesting anything Todd said, but I did understand that Bridget would eventually need to take a test to see if she carried genes associated with breast cancer, commonly known in the medical world as BRCA1 and BRCA2. These test results would glean more information about her family history and allow our kids and even our grandkids to see if they were at increased risk.

"I know this is a lot of information," Todd chuckled self-consciously. "Look, man, I know this is a difficult time. If there is ever anything I can do to help, I'm here for you."

We shook hands. I took his business card and knew I would probably be in touch at some point. Todd was married and had a boy Jack's age, so I knew if I wasn't contacting him for advice about genetic testing or a breast cancer-related issue, I would be calling to do something together with our families.

Only a couple hours after Bridget's diagnosis, I felt overwhelmed with information overload and a newfound sort of extra-sensory perception, yet I was learning about the importance and meaning of human connections, or in the case with Todd, reconnections. It was good to see my old buddy, albeit rather awkward and emotional.

As I walked away and opened the car door, I heard Todd call out to me. He had his hand by his ear as if he were holding a phone. "Call if I can do anything," he said.

# THE INSIDER

\* \* \*

Thursday at Dr. K's office had been the worst, most stressful day of my life—that is, until Friday, when we visited the hospital for a full barrage of tests to see whether Bridget's cancer had metastasized. She would undergo an MRI, bone scan, and CT scan all in the same day to reveal whether the cancer had spread to the most critical areas, including her brain, bones, lungs, and liver. One of the biggest frustrations, particularly for Bridget, was the fact that we would not learn the results from the tests until sometime early the following week. That would give us an entire weekend to brood over Bridget's fate, and that of our family. I knew that, as much as it would pain me, it would torment Bridget tenfold.

Everyone with whom we came in contact at the hospital could not have been nicer, but it did not make the situation any better. The male nurse who registered Bridget for her tests was very friendly. A tall man built like a linebacker, he was emotionally moved upon learning about her diagnosis.

"I'm sorry," he said, pausing in reflective silence. He seemed flustered and upset. Soon he regrouped himself and said, "You'll do just fine. It's amazing how far medicine has advanced."

He had covered himself nicely, but those words "I'm sorry" stuck with me. If medicine had made such advances, why did he need to say he was "sorry"? I did not fault the man, for he was truly sympathetic. Rather, I was disturbed by the utterly pervasive and unnerving stigma attached to the "C" word.

After Bridget went in for her first test, I quickly became claustrophobic in the cramped waiting room. My claustrophobia was, in turn, amplified by my own self-pity. As I looked at the others around me, I assumed they were there for reasons far less significant or severe. *That woman over there probably sprained her pinky*, I thought, *and that man over there is probably waiting for his son who has a bad case of gas. They don't know our lives are on the line.* As I waited for Bridget, I closed my eyes with my head facing down, resting on clenched fists. I could not bear to look at anybody.

My self-pity instantly disappeared when Bridget came into the waiting room in hysterics after her test. She was on the verge of collapse, having endured the emotional stress of learning of her life-threatening disease and contemplating how we would be affected, and now unsure of the severity of it all and feeling at the mercy of machines that would scan her body and dictate our fate. Together, we teetered on the brink. I watched in agony my lovely wife all puffy-eyed and out of breath, sobbing and speechless. *Somebody help us! Get a doctor!* I wanted to scream. But we were already at the hospital and nobody could give her a magical pill to make the disease disappear and heal her emotional wounds.

Any sense of privacy was left at the door when we entered the hospital. As I held Bridget in my arms, I felt helpless. By now, everybody had surely, intuitively assumed Bridget had that awful, dreadful, deadly disease that began with the letter "C."

"Let's just get through these next two tests," I told her. "Take it one step at a time."

Thankfully, I was allowed in the same room with Bridget during her final test, the bone scan. They were all important tests, but we knew this one would be critical. A clear bone scan would offer hope that the cancer had not metastasized.

The nurse administering the test helped to put Bridget at ease with something that seemed so unattainable at the time—normal conversation. Michelle was a young brunette with a natural effervescence. She and Bridget volleyed back and forth on topics ranging from sewing and dance to nutrition and kids as I stood by like a spectator watching a tennis match, my head moving from left to right, right to left. It was almost dizzying, and in any other case I would have either fallen asleep or left the room, but Michelle had provided the perfect elixir, an ounce of normalcy in a time when our universe had been unalterably knocked out of whack. The bone scan was a relatively long test, but we didn't seem to mind the added time with our new best friend.

After the test, we were sitting alone on a small bench in the hallway waiting for Bridget to be discharged. We felt stunned and shaken, as if we were students who had just turned in a test that we knew we had failed because we had had no time to prepare or study.

Michelle passed by in the hallway a couple of times, and we made eye contact. I knew she sensed our pain and burden, but she did not show it. Though she was young, she knew how to handle such a delicate situation with veteran ease and comfort. After a half-hour of waiting, Michelle hurriedly approached and sat next to us.

"Hey," she whispered to Bridget, smiling and winking. "I have a good feeling about your scan."

She was not supposed to tell us any of the results. That would be up to the radiologist to inform the oncologist, who would provide us with the official update. However, we knew what she was insinuating.

I grabbed Bridget and clutched her tightly, burying my face in her shoulders. I had held my emotions in check until then. The tears flowed, drowning out any understandable utterance. Thankfully Bridget was able to muster a few words of gratitude to Michelle, but I was simply unable.

We had been falling off the precipice, but now hung by a thread of hope.

# MADISON SQUARE GARDEN

## * * *

We had originally planned on celebrating Bridget's birthday in Orlando, where we were to visit her younger brother. Bridget was very close with Brian, who had recently moved to Florida, so she had been anxious to see him and his wife Corrina in their new home and take our boys to Disney World. While I had never been to Disney World or had the urge to see Mickey Mouse in person, I had been looking forward to the trip, which was to coincide with the installation of hardwood floor in our house. Several weeks earlier, our washing machine had malfunctioned and flooded part of our main level, ruining much of the floor. In a perfect world, we would have enjoyed the trip to Florida and arrived home to the new hardwood floor.

When we learned of Bridget's diagnosis, we cancelled the trip. Dr. K said that we could still go to Orlando as planned, as it would precede the start of her chemo treatment, but we decided to go another time when our spirits were intact. We did, however, move forward with the contract work, which meant our house would be uninhabitable for several days. We would be living at her mom and Dave's house during that time. Coping with a wife just diagnosed with cancer and living at the mother-in-law's could be hell. But for me, it was not bad. It would be a disruption to our normal routine, but by now we were becoming used to disruptions.

Sandy was not the stereotypical mother-in-law, in part because she was non-intrusive, almost to a fault, but primarily since she was so close to Bridget and our kids. She and Dave lived nearby and enjoyed keeping Jack and Andrew for sleepovers. Sandy was a counselor at the local public high school, and her twin sister, Suzy, was also a high school counselor. The two were inseparable. They talked with one another on the phone several times a day, vacationed together, and since they lived near one another regularly took walks in the neighborhood together. Sandy and Suzy also enjoyed painting, something from which Bridget and I benefited considerably, as they had painted much of the interior of our house. A staunch conservative, Sandy held strong political views and Christian values, as did Dave. She awoke early every morning to read the Bible and walk.

Sandy joined us at Bridget's first oncologist appointment. We were both armed with pens and notepads, ready to record every word from the doctor. It was reassuring to have Sandy with us, both for support and as another set of ears.

The first thing I noticed about the doctor was his long, flowing hair, like that of a mad scientist or a stylish Spanish hombre, depending on your take. But, after our first consultation with the oncologist, which lasted two full hours, we knew he was the right doctor, and thereafter we referred to him as El Hombre. He was honest, straightforward, and patient. In fact, he had offered to call my brother Matt, who was a doctor, to discuss Bridget's case in more detail for our own peace of mind. Unlike me, Matt, an urologist, had inherited the intelligent genes. I always admired him and valued his opinion, so it made me feel good knowing that he could learn about Bridget's case and treatment plan directly from the oncologist.

El Hombre confirmed that Bridget's cancer had not metastasized, or spread, to anywhere in her body beyond her lymph nodes. Her case was pretty severe, but it could have been worse. We would know more about the cancer the following week when a thorough examination of her biopsy was complete. Then Bridget would begin with chemotherapy, and the doctor would tell us the details of the treatment plan, which he assumed would also include surgery and radiation.

When we returned home from the hospital, we had hoped to relax and spend time with Jack and Andrew. Instead, we were greeted by one frustrated contractor, two crabby boys, and two overwhelmed relatives who were watching the boys. Days earlier, I had ripped up the old flooring in the living room and entryway to save on labor costs. Overnight, the living room became one large cavernous space with nothing but a subfloor, making it a perfect play area for the boys, who had taken it upon themselves to create their own hockey version of Madison Square Garden. Andrew played the part of Mark Messier and Jack that of Brian Leetch. Armed with hockey sticks, they shot the tennis ball, their version of a puck, back and forth across the family room, pretending to skate gracefully across smooth ice as they ran barefoot over the uneven, splinter-ridden subfloor.

Just as we walked in, Jack smashed his big toe while chasing the ball. His shriek quickly reached a piercing, feverish pitch. The contractor was pacing back and forth, distressed by the chaos as he took measurements for the job. Bridget's aunt and grandma were attempting to make us dinner, frantically looking for the pots and pans and ingredients for macaroni and cheese. In all the commotion and everybody instantaneously screaming for attention, I sat at the kitchen table, spent, speechless, and inwardly fuming. It was Bridget who needed the most attention, yet barrier after barrier stood in the way.

Moreover, I became doubly frustrated watching her relatives make our meal when I knew I was more than capable. We were losing control of our lives and independence.

"Mr. DuMont," the contractor called from the other room. "I've got some questions."

Just before Bridget's diagnosis, we had been deciding which kind of hardwood floor we wanted. Now, as he worked with his tape measurer, he needed to know our final selections for the type and width and finish of wood.

"I need to know now so I can place the order," he insisted.

Bridget was reading a flyer she had received from a woman we met at the hospital who ran a support center for cancer patients. The woman was nice and well intentioned but overwhelmed us with information and opportunities for Bridget, speaking with the speed of an auctioneer about cancer seminars and support groups and cosmetic tips and directions on how to shop for the right wig. The calendar on the flyer was filled nearly every day of the week with another "opportunity."

"There's a support group meeting tomorrow night," Bridget said. "Should I go?"

I did not want her to go because I knew she would be at the hospital often enough. Mostly, though, I just wanted to be with her, but I felt awkward saying it in front of her relatives. I simply did not want our lives to change so abruptly and drastically with so little time at home together.

"I would wait a few days," I said.

"Mr. DuMont," the contractor called again, now clearly out of patience.

I asked him for his recommendation, and without hesitation, I said, "Sounds great."

Then I moved on to tending to our boys, Bridget, and our resident cooks.

# MARATHON MAN

*** 

Though only a few days had passed since Bridget's diagnosis, it seemed we had lived a few months of our lives filled with stress, uncertainty, and chaos. The negatives, however, had been tempered by the blessings and support from friends, family, colleagues, and complete strangers. Several out-of-towners flew in to see Bridget, including her dad, her brother and sister-in-law, and a friend from college. My parents were due to arrive from Virginia the next weekend. I just wanted to be alone with Bridget and the boys, selfish as it may have been, but I was quickly learning that I would have to share her with others as we endured this struggle. The privacy in our lives that I had once cherished was quickly coming undone.

The dozens of phone messages we received each day, though tremendously thoughtful, became overwhelming. Frequently we had to take the phone off the hook just so we could talk to each other. Unlike Bridget, I never had a fondness for chit-chatting on the phone, and even she found returning all of the calls daunting, if not impossible. When a friend told us about a free online service for people in Bridget's situation, I was relieved. I quickly set up an account for Bridget on CaringBridge, which provided personalized websites that support and connect loved ones during critical illness, treatment, and recovery. Within days, the phone calls dwindled. Everybody had been receiving our updates through her CaringBridge site.

The support was truly incredible. Our family and friends stepped up in ways we never imagined. We received dinners and gift cards to restaurants and grocery stores and gas stations. My parents paid for a home cleaning service. Bridget's sister set up an online care calendar to organize dinners for our family. Our parents helped pay for our mounting medical expenses, and the student council at my school also helped with our financial burden by giving us a two-hundred-dollar check. I was doubly impressed and grateful for the students' support because I worked primarily with the alumni and knew only a handful of students at the school.

The Superior of our school's Jesuit community celebrated Mass in honor of Bridget and our family. It was a morning Mass before school on a Tuesday. Sitting near the front of the chapel, I did not realize how many had attended the ceremony until Communion, when, one after another, dozens of teachers and students filed by. Some winked at me, some patted me on my shoulder, and some simply passed in prayerful reflection. My hair stood on end.

An alumnus named Frank, who was in his early seventies and whom I knew only from a few brief encounters, called me at home one evening.

"Hey, Ben," he said, "I'm awfully sorry to bother you by calling you at home, but I wanted to see if it's okay if our prayer group at our parish says a Novena in your wife's honor."

Our conversation was brief. He was not interested in talking long. He just wanted to let me know that he cared. I was overcome with gratitude. I would see Frank a few times a year as he was on the school's Alumni Board, and when we talked he would always ask, "How's your wife?"

When I told him she was well, he would say "Good, good," immediately followed by, "You been biking much?" and we would talk about cycling and running. The man, shorter, with sharp features and light flowing hair, was an avid runner, still running marathons after completing forty of them over the course of his life. He had just finished a forty-mile off-road run in the mountains of North Carolina. "My back's been giving me trouble," Frank would say, and he would give me the latest on his health.

While I was moved by the love, prayers, and support from our family and friends, I was still too caught up in the emotion of our circumstance to fully realize and appreciate that God was working through them. I felt somewhat conflicted inside with confusion, anger, and a sense of abandonment. The words of Jesus in His darkest hour resonated in my mind: "My God, my God, why have you forsaken me?"

# MY FORTRESS

\* \* \*

I was leaving work and walking toward the parking lot through the basement corridor, a dark, unfinished area of the school that included storage rooms, the boiler room, and custodial and maintenance office space. The building was nearly a hundred years old, and the basement looked every bit its age amid the dim light and musty odor.

My eyes were bloodshot from insomnia and stress, and my head pounded with a migraine. It seemed every night I struggled to get to sleep, and when I was finally able to do so, I would awake before sunrise, my heart racing and my mind in a fog of worry and discontent. Six days after Bridget's diagnosis, I was nearing my threshold. I had wasted precious energy putting on the façade that everything would be okay, but inside it was tearing me up. Confusion, indecision, and fear had grabbed hold of my psyche. Clad in the lonely, forlorn rags of the unknown, I was spent and had no game plan.

"Ben!" somebody called from behind. The voice was loud and stern.

I was solely focused on getting to the parking lot as soon as possible so I could speed home and attempt to relax and ease the pressure in my head. Thus I pretended to ignore the man and kept on moving.

He called again. I turned around and saw Isaac, who was approaching quickly. As he neared, I realized that it was the first time he had ever called me by my name.

Without any prompting or introduction, he immediately began talking. "Hey, Ben, I know what you're feeling, man. I've been there, I know the hurt, brother, but you've got to stay strong, you know, man, both of you, you and your wife must turn to God." The words rolled off his tongue naturally, definitively, with conviction. The more he talked, the faster his words unraveled. "I've been there and back, man. I know what it's like. I just had cancer all over my mid-section less than a year ago.

"It was tough, but I turned to God, man, and after they sliced my whole mid-section wide open and did comprehensive surgery the cancer was wiped away, nothing left, not one thing. It was the Spirit, the Spirit wiped the cancer clear away, and after they stitched me back up I didn't need any pain medication because I let the Spirit come upon me. I let the Spirit come into me, right here, man, you see..." He pointed at his stomach. "...and I could feel no pain, man, still can feel no pain. I feel peace, brother, nothing but peace." He became louder and more impassioned as he spoke, gesturing like an orchestra conductor. His eyes remained fixed on mine, as if they were peering into my soul. "You have to let the Spirit come into you both, my brother, you must, because when you do the cancer will have no chance, the Spirit will wipe it clean away, so don't think about the cancer any more, man, no more, leave that to the doctors. You've got to turn to God."

After we shook hands and parted, I felt the same as I had when I left the office, utterly fatigued and frustrated. My mind was still numb from the stress and unable to absorb the simplicity and magnitude of what Isaac had told me. Part of me was annoyed. *Why did he insist on going out of his way to drag me to the side after such a long week and take up my time, time I desperately needed to spend with my wife and kids, time I needed to try and get some much-needed rest? And, of course, we all know we need to turn to God. Did he not know I was a follower of Christ and attended Mass regularly and prayed every morning and night?*

The impact of what Isaac said didn't strike me until I reached home, where I crashed on our couch in the middle of the living room, a veritable sawdust bowl with power tools and scrap wood scattered about, sheets of clear plastic hanging from the ceiling in between the rooms.

"What's the matter?" Bridget asked.

The boys were at Sandy's, and for the first time since her diagnosis our house was quiet. I was so enveloped in thought that I could not speak. For the past week I had been bent on trying to learn as much as possible about breast cancer and especially where Bridget fit in terms of survival rates. According to my online research, she fit somewhere in the range of a sixty percent survival rate. If I were betting, perhaps I would bet on her, but I was her husband, and I was frightened. Forty percent somehow seemed a far greater—and scarier—number than sixty percent. Even though the odds were somewhat in her favor, much of the online information was negative and upsetting. I knew it would not be easy and much would be sacrificed for her survival, regardless of the outcome. There had to be something more I could do to help her. Surely there was a better doctor somewhere, a better hospital, or anything that would improve her odds of survival. She had to be there for the boys, to watch them grow older, and to live with us well into the future. That was the plan. *How could any of us possibly go on without her, especially the boys?* I wondered. But the more I searched, the more frustrated I had become. The cynicism and pessimism of the endless websites and blogs had put a stranglehold on me.

"Ben, are you okay?"

Then I thought about Isaac. I distilled his impassioned speech, every last one of his rhapsodic words into one simple message: *Don't worry about the cancer. That's up to the doctors. Let go and turn to God.* I literally felt the Holy Spirit come upon me in one great, overwhelming wave of relief. A switch suddenly flicked within me, leaving the despondency in the darkness.

"Honey, what is it?" Bridget asked again, sympathetically, her concern turning to worry.

Finally I looked at her. Then I embraced her and began to cry.

"It's all good," was all I could muster at first, to allay her worry. "Everything's gonna be okay. I'm so relieved."

"Well, that's great, honey," she said, seeming almost as relieved as I was. "But, what happened?"

As I told her about Isaac, I could see his eyes, those intense, beaming eyes that spoke of sickness and sadness and the triumphant power of the Holy Spirit. They moved me to tears, shed no longer from fear or despair, but from hope and happiness in knowing that we would prevail. The odds suddenly seemed stacked in our favor.

"There is no alternative," I said. "We're going to fight this, and we're going to win. We can beat anything."

From that point, our attitude began to take on a distinctive shift, something I wrote about on Bridget's CaringBridge site.

Part of a journal entry included:

...Now Bridget and I both feel the relief. Our attitude has been transformed, and our outlook is overwhelmingly positive. Those moments of fear, question, and doubt we experienced the first few days have made us stronger...because the fear, question, and doubt have been quashed by the knowledge that we will prevail. I am proud of Bridget's persistence, spirit, and will to overcome this disease, which has become more of an inconvenience than a monster. In fact, one day we will feel blessed by this momentary "inconvenience."

Another excerpt:

Looking back, the first week after learning "the news" was definitely the most difficult. Since then, as I've written, our attitude has completely shifted…thanks in large part to the support from friends and family…and even strangers. Day by day we have grown stronger, and our faith has grow in ways I never imagined. Incredibly, the frustration, doubt, and fear we initially experienced have transformed to peacefulness, and our hope has become unwavering confidence. At times, I find it difficult to see the fear in others when they show their care and concern. Simply, there is nothing to fear when you place yourself entirely in the hands of God…anything is attainable. As we continue to plod forward, we focus upward…

I ended with a Bible passage:

My soul finds rest in God alone;
My salvation comes from him.
He alone is my rock and my salvation;
He is my fortress, I will never be shaken.
PSALM 62:1-2

The power and intensity of Isaac's message reminded me of a pep talk I heard when I played football in high school. Our team was losing at halftime in the state semifinals. The mood in the locker room was one of utter deflation, until our assistant coach shook the walls with a motivational talk for the ages. He was a big man with an even bigger voice, a man who could unleash an intimidating presence on a dime. Though I cannot recall his exact words, I vividly remember how he transformed the spirit of the entire team. When we stepped onto the field for the third quarter, we knew we were going to win. There was no debate. It was a foregone conclusion that we would win, and we did.

Though I wasn't playing for a state championship now, I was in a bigger game with far greater consequences. My game plan called for me to be a supportive husband and good father, but that wasn't enough. I wanted to do more. Somehow, I wanted to manifest the compelling inner strength imparted by Isaac, whose impassioned words and deep eyes were really conduits for the Holy Spirit. I now felt driven by my faith, and not my life. Isaac made me realize that we were not victims. We were, indeed, in a fight, and our reaction would dictate not only our direction, but more importantly, our fate.

My responsibilities, which were already plentiful at home, proliferated. Days after my encounter with Isaac, I was still physically defeated from overexertion, stress, and lack of sleep. I consistently awoke at 4 A.M. and could not get back to sleep. One of my coping mechanisms was to plow ahead with the daily chores. I would frequently be doing dishes or folding laundry after 11 P.M. Yet throughout the physical distress, I felt strong and blessed to have an undaunted faith and the love of friends and family. I could deal with being tired.

With my newfound attitude and seemingly boundless spiritual strength, I began to keep a journal on our laptop. I found solace in writing my innermost thoughts and feelings.

Some journal excerpts:

Cancer is not a death sentence; it's a life sentence that compels you to live life to the fullest.

\* \* \*

Cancer has a way of breaking you down but for a moment, then building you up. Really, cancer is its own worst enemy.

\* \* \*

Life is not a riddle to be unraveled, but rather a mystery at which we must marvel.

\* \* \*

God is powerful and almighty and loves me infinitely. What shall I do in return?

As the days turned to weeks, I felt the need to harness and channel this spiritual fervor. I spent a fair amount of time in my car driving to and from work, about thirty miles each way. During this time, insulated from the world, music became more than just an outlet. I had a large collection of CDs I enjoyed listening to, many of them alternative mixes that my brother and I traded back and forth. Matt and I shared a passion for music, and thankfully, similar taste. Music became an opportunity for me to visualize the annihilation of Bridget's cancer. There was no anger or self-pity or self-doubt when I listened to the tunes; instead, my total being was focused on wiping away the cancer through visualization. At other odd moments, too, I would envision the chemotherapy drugs doing their devastating work on the cancer. Visualization became an important avenue for me to exercise the spiritual intensity that I felt.

At work, I would occasionally sneak away from the noise of the school to the peace of the small chapel. Unlike the school's main chapel, it was rarely used and only seated a few dozen. The back wall faced west and on it there was a pretty stained glass window of the North American Martyrs, eight Jesuit missionaries who were brutally tortured and killed in the mid-seventeenth century while working with the Huron Indians in Canada. There I would thank God for the gift of my wife and family, for my faith, and the fact that we had health insurance and access to medicine and caring, knowledgeable doctors. I would pray silently in reflective, repetitive fashion before heading back to the office.

Indeed, Isaac's advice to "turn to God" now resonated within our daily lives. Bridget became keenly interested in learning more about our faith and Scripture. She made plans to join a Bible study group when her health and schedule allowed. One evening, Bridget suddenly grabbed my attention as she read from her Bible.

"Babe, you have to listen to this," she said. "You won't believe it."

From a footnotes section, she read about the Biblical character Isaac: "In a family of forceful initiators, Isaac was the quiet 'mind-my-own business' type unless he was specifically called on to take action."

I thought of Isaac's words of encouragement and thanked God for his presence in my life. Smiling, I said, "That sounds like the Isaac I know."

# KEE-KEE

* * *

While our attitude and outlook had made a significant reversal, we were still human, and with Easter approaching, we continued to pray for our own miracle, hopelessly seeking the resurrection of our former lives. Thoughts of the boys growing old without their mommy plagued our minds. These notions of doom and gloom were accentuated at a local Easter egg hunt. It was our first social appearance after Bridget's diagnosis.

Rain from the prior evening on a cold, cloudy spring day had left behind a gigantic puddle-dotted field highlighted by hundreds of yellow, blue, green, pink, and orange plastic eggs. The egg hunt, held at a nearby school and sponsored by the local Chamber of Commerce, featured concessions, live music, various games for the kids, and an assortment of clowns, including one who towered and teetered above the rest on stilts. Nearly all of Bridget's family was there, including Sandy, Dave, Bridget's grandma, aunt, brother, sister, nieces, and nephews. Hundreds of eager, colorfully clad children met at the start line, which stretched for several dozen yards. They were accompanied by their coddling, camera-toting parents. Smiles abounded, and all seemed bereft of any pain, strife, or ailment. It was hard for me to put on a happy face. I longed for the days when we were like the other parents whose only dilemma was determining what color plaid their kids would wear for the egg hunt.

Andrew had been talking about the Easter egg hunt for days. He was only one, and though most kids his age didn't talk much, he instantly became a chatterbox when the topic was candy. In fact, he was susceptible to getting the shakes when he didn't have sugar. I envisioned him running all over the field and knocking over the other kids like a running back bent on reaching the end zone. Jack, on the other hand, had a different motive. It wasn't the goodies inside the eggs he was interested in as much as the number of eggs he would snag. He had spent hours strategizing how he could collect more eggs than anybody else. Such was the dichotomy of our boys, two unique and diametrically opposing personalities that could form the perfect collaborative balance. If they were a tandem in a fighter jet, Jack would be navigating and mapping the precise coordinates of the enemy, while Andrew would have control of the Gatling gun and fire away in crazed, unrelenting fashion. Nonetheless, they both possessed the same highly competitive spirit, and the egg hunt provided the ideal outlet.

When the whistle blew to begin the hunt, the throng of kids sprang upon the field like a school of piranha on some helpless prey. I shadowed Andrew as Bridget followed Jack. We were separate but nearby, and occasionally Bridget and I made eye contact. We smiled in a forced kind of way. She was wearing sunglasses to hide her puffy, blood-shot eyes. Earlier she was brought to tears after imagining this as her last Easter with us. I had been too busy and preoccupied since her diagnosis to even begin to realize, from her perspective, the weight and impact of it all. I had been in survival mode, and now as I saw her walking amid the smiling flock of humanity in her despondent state, she seemed immensely fragile and vulnerable, and my heart bled with empathy for her. I thought about when we first met, the innocence of her smile, the selflessness of her spirit, and the fervor of our love, and tears began to well in my eyes. Then I thought about the first time I told her I loved her, that sunny Valentine's day near the coast of California in wine country.

A few minutes into the hunt, she brought Jack over to me and said she was going to the car. She needed some time alone. It was too much—the sight of all the kids and smiles and families and the sounds of laughter and, inevitably, the thought of our boys, our family without her.

"Dad, where's Mom?" Jack asked after she had left for the car.

I wondered how many more times my boys would ask me that perilous question.

"She had to go get something from the car," I replied. "She'll be back soon."

*And how many times,* I thought, *will I tell the boys something just to buy time, distract them, or just flat out lie to them?*

I knew I could handle the sacrifice of being a caregiver to Bridget—in fact, I saw it as an honor and privilege, more than simply a duty—but I was unsure if our boys could tolerate seeing her endure such pain. They were too young, too innocent to deal with such a complex issue and not knowing if they would have a mom next year. None of it seemed fair. I shuddered when they asked, "Is Mommy going to be okay?"

After all of the eggs had been collected, we walked to meet Bridget's family at the picnic tables for lunch. Along the way, I ran into several friends, neighbors, and old acquaintances. Their first question was always, "Where's Bridget?" I had become used to telling people what had happened, but it was the first time I had to do so in front of the kids. We had been forthright with telling our boys that Bridget was sick and she was going to see the doctor to get better, but I could tell they were quickly becoming overwhelmed, as I was, by the questions, concerns, and reactions of others. I was walking a tightrope in balancing our own openness with the well-wishers and the well-being of our children, particularly Jack. Andrew was still very young and unable to grasp the concept of cancer, while Jack's advanced three-year-old mind, perpetually inquisitive and acutely sensitive, posed an ongoing challenge for Bridget and me. Jack seemed to have bionic ears and the memory of an elephant. He would recall things he had heard as a one-year-old and recite them with flawless precision. While we encouraged our boys to ask us questions, I knew Jack was soaking in our conversations with others and only hoped it would not have any detrimental effect.

Jen, one of our old neighbors, stopped me just before we reached the concession area. We were near a pair of supersized speakers blaring pop music.

"Hey, Ben, where's Bridget?" she asked. Her tone had already suggested something was wrong, as if a mom without her boys at an Easter egg hunt was a crisis in and of itself.

"She's here, somewhere," I replied, my eyes scanning the crowd by the field. I was carrying Jack with one hand, and holding Andrew's hand with the other. I was frequently toting Jack as of late, as his injured toe made it hard for him to walk.

"What?" she shouted over the music.

"I don't know," I yelled back, straining a grin.

"How's she been?"

"She's been better..." I began to say before Jen cut me off with another "What?" Meanwhile, Jack was complaining about his toe.

"She's got cancer," I said, loud enough for her to hear.

She reacted as if I had told her Bridget had just passed away. Most people were surprised and shocked when they heard the news for the first time, but Jen began to cry and go into a diatribe about how it was unfair and not possible and on and on. It was more than I could bear. I was holding Mr. Ears, and he was listening and taking it all in. We still had not had "the talk" with Jack—or Andrew, though we were less concerned about him because of his age—and wanted our own shock to dissipate a little before we did so. He knew that Mommy had been going to the hospital for some tests and that she may be sick, but we were trying to protect him for a little longer until we learned more about Bridget's cancer and treatment plan. Instinctively, I blew by Jen.

"She's gonna get better," I said, patting her on the shoulder. "I've got to go find her."

I felt like a walking shadow in the wake of Bridget's diagnosis, and now more so than ever. At first, it was as if I had to share her. People were eager to know how she was doing. They wanted to see her. But after just a few days of her diagnosis, everywhere I went—every time—everybody wanted to know about Bridget. That was the way it should have been, of course. All of the focus and prayers needed to be on her. I appreciated everybody's care and concern for Bridget, but they were constant reminders of how much of our lives, our energy, and our time revolved around her illness, and how, ultimately, cancer was a family disease that deeply affected all loved ones. No longer did people ask about me, and only occasionally about the boys. It was not attention or sympathy that I needed. I simply longed for the way things used to be. I wanted to have a conversation unrelated to illness or difficulty, and I wanted my dear lovely wife to complain about something mundane like a sore back or car traffic—anything other than dread of chemotherapy or fear of dying.

Bridget returned from the car soon after we met her family for lunch. She still wore her sunglasses, and her mood had not lightened. The kids played with their trinkets and ate candy as the rest of us tried to enjoy eating cold hot dogs and tried harder to pretend that all would be okay amid forced conversation and blaring music. It was apparent Jack was taking on our mood. The more the morning dragged on, the more he clung to our sides and the more sullen he became.

We drove home emotionally drained, though we knew we had chalked up one small victory. After the Easter egg hunt, nearly everybody we knew was aware of Bridget's condition. Sometimes it seemed telling people was nearly as hard as first hearing the news of her diagnosis ourselves. By going to the egg hunt, we had succeeded in trying to maintain a sense of normalcy in our lives, and Jack and Andrew were thrilled with their mounds of candy.

As we continued trying to resume our daily routines, I gradually realized the magnitude of Bridget's inner strength, her sheer will power to plow through our day-to-day activities without letting cancer dictate what we did or did not do. Her mother had told her that our kids would react to the cancer in the same manner that we did. It was great advice from a great woman, and those sage words moved Bridget. She made it her commitment to not let the kids see her cry or see her down, and to continue with life as we once did, to the greatest extent possible.

The following day, Easter Sunday, proved to be a blissful distraction from the stress and anxiety. The Easter Bunny brought Jack a new Superman shirt, and I told him he could wear it to church in place of his oxford under his vest. It clashed with his plaid pants, but I said he would look like the real Superman that way. He was convinced and walked around all puffy-chested, while Bridget bit her lip and ultimately couldn't help but laugh and go along with it. By the end of the day, Andrew had succeeded in consuming an entire chocolate bunny and most of his candy-filled eggs. Bridget's spirits were high most of the day, particularly after Sandy shared with her a Bible passage. It was a verse from John 11:4, one which she had randomly opened her Bible to that morning: "When Jesus heard that, He said, this sickness is not unto death but for the glory of God, that the Son of God may be glorified through it."

We had had some knowledge and experience with Scripture and spirituality, but now they were becoming intertwined with our everyday lives, our innermost movements, thoughts, and feelings. The power of prayer took on new and added meaning, and we took an interest in learning more about the Bible. A copy of the book now rested on my nightstand, and Bridget was talking to friends about forming a Bible study group.

We also hugged our kids a little harder and told them we loved them more often. This was easy to do after the Easter festivities had concluded and the boys were getting ready for bed. Andrew was unable to say "candy" and referred to it instead as "kee-kee." He took his bag of candy to his room and placed it beside his bed, as if to protect it from some nighttime sugar bandits.

Proud and smiling, he looked at his mound of candy and said, "I got my kee-kee."

# HERCEPTIN

*** 

The day after Easter, Bridget underwent surgery to implant a port, which would be used to administer the chemotherapy, in her upper chest. The procedure went fine, but she was taking a couple different types of pain medication and became nauseated and irritable when we returned to Sandy and Dave's house, our temporary residence while our new flooring was being installed. In the evening, Bridget grew upset and emotional when she was unable to put Andrew in his crib because of her pain and soreness. For the first time, her condition had come between her and the kids.

"I don't know how I'm going to do this," she said, sobbing.

Thankfully, Jack provided some levity in the midst of the day's gloom. My parents were in town and had taken care of the boys while we were at the hospital earlier in the day. Jack nearly sent my dad to the hospital after he picked up some handcuffs at the dollar store, put them on my dad, then conveniently lost the key. I did not know how they finally broke the handcuffs, but my dad's wrists were pretty scuffed up. It helped to lighten the mood in the evening, as Jack and my dad could not stop laughing about the whole ordeal.

The following day Bridget began her chemotherapy. Relative to her port surgery, it was easy. I had envisioned chemo as a painful process, but I soon learned that it was only painful for a few days after the drugs were administered. Bridget sat in a reclining chair alongside several other patients also receiving chemotherapy. It reminded me of a barber shop with all of the chairs lined up and the nurses administering to and chatting idly with the patients, though the setting was more stale and sterile, the mood more sullen. It was painless for Bridget, even boring. Not long after her chemo began, she fell asleep, in large part due to the heavy dose of Benadryl she received to avert an allergic reaction.

We spoke at length with the oncologist about the final test results, which concluded that Bridget's cancer was manifest in multiple tumors about four centimeters in diameter in her left breast and lymph nodes. The tumors were stage III of IV, indicating they were fairly advanced. Her specific type of can-cer—HER2-positive—contained a protein that promoted the development of cancer cells, meaning it was aggressive and fast growing. It also meant the doctors could better target and treat the cancer with a new, innovative drug called Herceptin, which had just been developed by a research doctor and approved by the FDA for use in early stages. Consequently, El Hombre revised his initial treatment plan. He had presented her case to the team of cancer specialists at the hospital, and they agreed on this modified, more aggressive treatment. Bridget would now receive chemotherapy for twenty-four weeks upfront, as opposed to sixteen weeks as originally scheduled, then have surgery, followed by radiation for six weeks. After radiation, Bridget would continue to receive Herceptin for another six months. Her entire treatment plan was now expected to last about eighteen months.

El Hombre felt optimistic about the approach and said the Herceptin provided added ammunition against the can-cer. The drug increased the possibility of making the cancer undetectable before surgery. This would be a best-case scenario, though the doctors planned to do surgery regardless of the size of the tumors. While HER2-positive breast cancer was less responsive to other hormone treatments, it did respond to Herceptin, which could slow the growth of the cancer and even decrease its size. Herceptin isolated cancer cells, essentially stopping their growth. The drug also attacked roaming or debris cancer cells that may have spread throughout the body. Using a war analogy, El Hombre said Herceptin would act like the Air Force striking key enemy communication hubs, disabling the enemy from its ability to strategize, regroup or strike back. Moreover, Herceptin had a synergistic effect when combined with standard chemotherapy drugs. Its effectiveness multiplied, much like the Army and Air Force uniting.

"Because this is an aggressive type of cancer, we will treat it accordingly," El Hombre told us, speaking with a cool calm, a subdued intensity. "We will use everything at our disposal and hope for a grand slam."

When he said this, I got goosebumps. I was moved, motivated, even inspired by his *you-wanna-play-hardball, we'll-play-hardball* attitude. He knew the stakes were high, and he was not messing around.

Herceptin had a few possible side effects, including heart problems in a small percentage of patients. Thus, Bridget would receive regular tests to ensure the drug was having no adverse effect on her heart. The following day she would receive her first MUGA heart scan—short for Multi-Gated Acquisition scan, a nuclear imaging test that evaluates the function of the heart—to establish her baseline. On the upside, we learned Herceptin did not cause patients to lose their hair, so after Bridget's twenty-four weeks of chemotherapy, her hair would begin to grow back.

El Hombre reiterated that we were lucky to have Herceptin at our disposal.

"If this would have happened to you a few years ago before Herceptin was available, you may very well have been out of luck," he said. "Now you have hope."

Herceptin or no Herceptin, we still felt out of luck. Nonetheless, it was reassuring to know we had something going for us, no matter how inconsequential it seemed. Bridget would get her chemo treatments every other Tuesday, a process that would typically take less than two hours. Each following day she would return to the hospital to get a shot to help with nausea. The doctor said the chemo treatments would not begin to fully impact Bridget for a couple of months, but then the cumulative effect of the poison would wreak havoc on her body.

When we returned home from the hospital, Bridget crashed, still feeling the effects of the Benadryl. The flooring work at our house was finally complete, and it felt good to be back home. My parents, my grandma, and my aunt had spent the entire day transforming our disorganized dustbowl of a house into a home again. The new floor looked great, and we were looking forward to getting settled back into a routine. My dad was leaving the following day, but my mom would be staying with us for a couple of weeks to help with everything at home.

A short while after we had been home, I heard a loud noise outside. It seemed to be coming from our front lawn. I peered out the window and saw our neighbor, Eric, cutting our grass. I knew he was not fond of yard work, and when I went out to tell him to stop, he insisted on finishing the job. Such was the kindness of our family, friends, and neighbors.

# BUZZ PARTY

### \* \* \*

Since Bridget's diagnosis, I continually wondered what we would tell the kids. How would we break the news to them, and how would they react? Her cancer did not affect them immediately, so we wanted to put if off, at least for several days. It felt good to protect them, even if it was for a short time, so we could tell them about her illness on our own terms.

Jack had been watching a movie when we first told him Bridget had cancer. I pressed pause on the DVD player, and we began our talk, which Bridget and I had rehearsed.

We said Mommy had a bump in her chest that was "icky" stuff called cancer, so she would have to go to the doctor a lot to get better and would often be tired and not feel well. With nervous anticipation, we awaited his response. We expected he, like others, would begin crying and wailing and cursing the heavens. However, Jack calmly looked at us without hesitation and asked if we could press play on the DVD player.

Bridget and I looked at each other and chuckled. We were relieved but knew that he was preoccupied and not comprehending what we were talking about. We had been particularly nervous about Jack's reaction given his sensitivity and awareness of the world around him.

Remembering Sandy's advice that our kids would react to the cancer in the same manner we did provided added motivation to set the right example for Jack and Andrew. Bridget resolved to have open dialogue and communication with everybody, especially our boys. She did not want her cancer to be something she would ever hide. She was fine with it being part of her new identity, but she was determined not to let it define or limit her. Through open lines of communication, she could confront her cancer with honesty, in addition to telling her story and spreading awareness for the disease.

Bridget also committed to become stronger by strengthening her faith. This became a focal point of her life, and in time our faith became the center of our lives together. I had felt somewhat deserted by God after Bridget's diagnosis, but in time I felt His presence, palpable and powerful, through our family, friends, and generous supporters. Any feelings of abandonment had waned and disappeared. As I had written in my journal, life, indeed, was not a "riddle to be unraveled, but rather a mystery at which we must marvel." Pain, suffering, disease, even death were perhaps the greatest mysteries of life, but I learned to embrace, not fight, these sorrowful wonders. God had not punished Bridget and our family with cancer, but He had given us an opportunity to do something special with it, something beyond merely surviving. He did not have an obligation to magically appear and make everything better in our lives; instead, I had a responsibility to be open to receiving His love, hope, and peace. With this openness I became more willing to be a beacon of God's light through my own thoughts, words, and actions. When we took the blame away from God, our religious and spiritual paradigms shifted. God was no longer at the top of a hierarchical structure or pyramid, but instead the center from which everything emanated.

Recognizing this changing dynamic, we became more aware of and grateful for all that we had.

We had a small chalkboard in our kitchen, and Bridget would regularly write Bible passages and other inspirational quotes on it. I particularly cherished one of them, which remained on the chalkboard for a long time because it focused on the Ignatian theme of gratitude. It read:

In happy moments, praise God.
In difficult moments, seek God.
In quiet moments, worship God.
In painful moments, trust God.
Every moment, thank God.

Our fresh spiritual perspective benefited our daily lives and relationships with others. Bridget had always been very close to her maternal grandma, who still lived nearby, and after her diagnosis we made an extra effort to visit Moe after Mass on the weekends and during the week with the boys. Bridget would pick up Moe to run errands with the boys, anything to spend time with her, sometimes visiting with her several times each week. Realizing the gifts God had bestowed on us provided added hope and resilience. Jack and Andrew, God's greatest gifts to us, at first seemed to add to our anxiety through Bridget's illness, but they became a consummate source of strength. Their innocence and humor gave us comfort and reassurance.

Faced with the inevitability of losing her hair, Bridget again recalled the advice her mother had given her that our boys would react to the cancer the same way she did. She did not want to lose her dignity when she lost her flowing blonde locks. Rather, she wanted it to make her—and others around her—stronger. She wanted her hair to come out on her own terms, instead of clump by clump on its own. And she wanted to have some fun with it for the sake of the kids. Shortly after her first chemo treatment, when her hair would begin to fall out, we decided to throw a "buzz party."

Lance, her hair stylist, had offered to shave her head at the salon when it was closed. Nearly all of Bridget's family— Sandy, Dave, Bridget's grandma, her aunt, brother, sister, cousins, niece, and all the nephews—convened on a Sunday afternoon to witness Bridget take on a new identity. She would become hairless yet retain her vigor and humor. Sandy brought Bridget's favorite treat, chocolate-covered strawberries, and donuts and juice for the kids, who ran about the salon like it was a playhouse, laughing and clowning as they took turns in the barber chairs, pretending to cut one another's hair, then acting like astronauts under the bulbous hair dryers. Without Bridget's knowing, Dave had his own head shaved at a nearby salon to show his support. When he arrived, Bridget greeted him with surprise and emotion, and the kids welcomed him with laughter and wisecracks.

Bridget gave Jack the scissors to make the ceremonial first cut. Lance held her hair taut, then Jack, giggling and looking around at everybody to make sure it was okay, snapped the scissors and the long-flowing strands of hair fell to the floor. Bridget smiled, and the kids erupted in laughter. Andrew, followed by the other kids and everybody else, took turns with the scissors. Then Lance made a few more cuts, and I helped him finish the job.

"I think you're having too much fun with this," Bridget joked, as I was reluctant to hand the clippers over to Lance after shaving a mohawk into Bridget's head.

"This could be the start of a new career for me," I said.

After she was bald, Bridget put on her new wig, and Lance cut it to her liking. He generously did everything free of charge.

Bridget admitted the "buzz party" was a bit of a gamble in terms of how the kids would react, and so we were relieved when Jack and Andrew left in a good mood and feeling comfortable with the fact that their mom no longer had a real head of hair. In fact, they liked how Bridget looked and preferred she not wear her wig. They would regularly tell her to take off her wig, and Andrew would rub her head and laugh with a contagious guttural giggle. Jack had several clown wigs, and when Bridget was wearing her wig he would put on one of his own multi-colored heads of hair. Bridget typically did not wear her wig around the house, and Jack felt fine if his friends came over and saw that his mom had no hair. She was good-looking with or without hair. I told her to be thankful for having no hair, for it meant the chemo was working on killing the cancer cells.

One night, Bridget went to bed early and Andrew saw her without her wig. He walked to her side and asked, "Hair go mama?" Then he ran over to her dresser, grabbed her wig and brought it to her. She put it on, and less than a second later he took it off, rubbed her head and laughed and ran away.

# DOGWOOD CANYON

* * *

A week before Memorial Day weekend, I took Bridget and the boys to Dogwood Canyon, a pristine, ten thousand-acre private park situated near Branson in southwest Missouri. It was part of a trip I had planned to Silver Dollar City, an amusement park that was essentially the Midwest's version of Disneyland, after we cancelled our trip to Florida. Bridget was upset about not traveling to see her brother Brian and his family, so I was hopeful that going to Branson would be more than a mere consolation trip.

We were relieved to get away and escape together. All of us were craving a sense of normalcy in our lives, something to take our minds off the worry and fear of Bridget's illness, anything to bring us back to the days before we heard the word "kiddo." Bridget was excited to do something outdoors, and the boys were eager to go bicycling, an activity we had enjoyed together since they were old enough to sit in a bike trailer. It had quickly become our favorite pastime.

The weather was perfect when we arrived, near eighty degrees and sunny with no humidity. We rented bikes at the park station, and Jack picked out the smallest one, which was about as tall as his shoulders.

"How old is he?" asked the park ranger.

"Three," I said, "but he'll be fine."

The man seemed hesitant about Jack riding on the trail and suggested he test the bike in the parking lot. I had to help Jack up because the bike was too tall for him to straddle. The handlebars were much wider than his at home, so it took him a few seconds to steady the bike, but once he had it under control he navigated the parking lot with ease, confidence, and a sly grin.

"Okay, I suppose he'll be fine," the park ranger agreed.

Jack had demonstrated an impressive sense of balance and coordination when he learned to walk at an early age. Similarly, he had shown interest, even skill, in riding a bike when he was one. He had frequented my bike races with Bridget and was my loudest cheerleader. In casual conversation, he would say, "When I grow up, I want to be like Eddy Merkz and ride so fast my helmet flies off." In his spare time, he practiced riding his bike on our back deck. Soon his tires and training wheels had worn an oval path, chipping the paint and splintering the wood. During the summer we would pretend he was racing. "One more lap to go, and it looks like Jack is going to win!" I would shout. "More, Daddy," he would say when it was over. "One more race."

The previous fall, when Jack was two, he had learned to ride without training wheels. I took him to a little-league baseball diamond near our house early one morning after the fall season was over. The sun was warm on our backs as we walked onto the field. An empty soda can clinked and clanged as it blew across the empty diamond, while a partial Big League Chew wrapper lay stuck, fluttering in the dugout fence like a fly trying to escape a spider web. A groundsman appeared from a small maintenance building near the outfield. He was the only one around. When he saw us, he stopped. He reached in his pocket, grabbed a cigarette and skillfully lit it, shielding the flame from the wind. Then he methodically took his first drag and stared at us.

"Daddy, you won't even have to hold on to me," said Jack stubbornly.

He rolled his little green bike onto the diamond and threw one leg over the frame.

"I can do it, Dad," he said, looking back at me.

I held him steady for the launch, pushed, and let go.

When I challenged myself to teach Jack how to ride his bike without training wheels at age two, I assumed I would become frustrated and disappointed. Nonetheless, I had high hopes. I set out, first and foremost, to build his confidence on training wheels. When his confidence was soaring, I would release him on the most ideal learning environment on two wheels, somewhere flat with a forgiving surface.

As I let go on the baseball diamond, Jack accelerated without hesitation. His feet spun frenetically, and he turned around to make sure I was not holding or chasing him. I stood motionless, excited, and stunned. I tried to restrain my exhilaration so as not to scare him, so I simply clapped and cheered in a subdued manner.

Then I heard somebody else clapping in the distance. It was the groundsman. He held his cigarette in his mouth as he clapped and raised his hands with fists of encouragement.

Tears of pride and happiness filled my eyes as I savored the next forty-five minutes watching Jack ride continuously, flawlessly through the infield, his tires carving skinny, circuitous paths covering nearly every inch of dirt by the time he had finished. Before we left to go home, he had already graduated to the parking lot.

Jack continued to blossom on the bike through the next spring, when Bridget was diagnosed. To help maintain consistency with his activities and our lives, I made a commitment to continue spending time with him on the bike. It was the perfect escape for us both.

As we set off from the ranger station in Dogwood Canyon, Andrew was in tow behind me in a trailer, sandwiched in between two full coolers and snuggled with his teddy bear. He constantly kept an eye on Jack to see who was ahead. Jack too seemed more interested in racing than soaking in the scenery, as he passed us immediately after we left the park station.

A stream cut through the canyon, and alongside the trail scores of rainbow trout were visible beneath the crystal-clear water. Towering oaks were interspersed throughout the expansive green space surrounded by hilly woods. Squirrels scampered about, up and down trees, several cutting across the bike path just in front of us, while rabbits flitted through the meadow that met an incline near the edge of the bank. At one point, a mink casually ambled alongside the path only a few feet away.

After several miles, we stopped and sat at a picnic table for lunch. It was next to the stream where a waterfall cascaded down from a canyon cliff. The sound of water was loud yet soothing, and the pool rippled outward, the fish darting beneath. We lay our spread on the table and tore into the sandwiches and chips and apples and sodas. It had been a good haul for us all. My body ached, but it felt good after towing the extra weight of Andrew and the coolers in the trailer.

"I'm so glad we did this," Bridget said.

"Me, too," I replied.

The boys echoed in unison, "Me, too, Mommy."

"We're glad we didn't go to Florida," Jack added. "We just want to stay here."

"I want to stay here," said the little one.

Bridget was happy to be outside for a change and doing something active in the fresh air; Jack was relieved to take a break after handling his oversized bike well through the park and up the slight hills; and Andrew was content to be along for the ride, though he really wanted to be biking as well.

A determined little guy, Andrew was perseverant, with a strong will, so much so that he would later be riding his own bike without training wheels at age two, just as his big brother had done. He thrived on competition and was constantly trying to keep up with Jack.

Andrew had a fondness for the mechanized world of planes, trains, and automobiles. In his estimation, the louder something was, the better. While most kids would cringe at the sound of a mufflerless automobile peeling out, Andrew would smile and laugh hysterically. A poster of the Blue Angels hung prominently in his bedroom. One day I asked him if he would prefer to be a Blue Angel or a Thunderbird, explaining that the Thunderbirds were basically the all-stars of the Air Force, and the Blue Angels were those of the Navy. "Thunderbird, Daddy," he said definitively, without hesitation. Thunderbird then became his nickname. Jack decided he needed a nickname as well. "Dad, call me Sharp Arrow," he said. The names stuck for a long while, and though I was never quite sure how Jack had come up with Sharp Arrow, the names fit them both well. Thunderbird beckoned thoughts of something fast and furious, much like the supersonic planes themselves, something intent on accomplishing its objective through sheer will, fearlessness, and determination, though at times erratic and unconventional. Sharp Arrow, conversely, carried connotations of intelligence, precision, and purpose, akin to a Native American of yore whittling away at his arrow, preparing and strategizing for the kill with his bow after conferring with his fellow warriors about tactics.

Sharp Arrow and Thunderbird wrestled in the grass near the stream after lunch. I had made a habit of taking them on hikes at a park near our house since they were babies, and I always referred to it as the "tree park." It was a place where we could bond with nature, a peaceful haven bereft of distractions, where we could interact freely and openly with one another. Now as they played together, giddy with excitement, Sharp Arrow said, "We really like this tree park."

Bridget and I found ourselves in a state of disbelief as we continued riding after lunch, reveling in the open air, glancing at each other and commenting, "Can you believe it?"

Finally, we seemed free from cancer. I did not have to share Bridget with others, and I was not walking in her shadow. We were carefree and together as a family doing what we had once taken for granted. Now, more than ever, I relished our time together.

I was constantly turning around and telling Sharp Arrow he was doing well, egging him on with words of encouragement to build his confidence.

"Good job, buddy," I said.

"Daddy, I'm Eddy Merkx," he said as he passed ahead of us, his little body bobbing up and down on the bike. He knew the former Belgian professional cyclist was widely considered to be the best of all time.

"Jack, you can't do that!" Thunderbird yelled from the trailer. "Dad, get him. Beat Jack."

After completing the eight-mile loop in the park, we returned our bikes to the ranger station, and the old man shook his head and chuckled at the sight of Jack.

On our way to our condo near Silver Dollar City, we passed a cemetery on the side of the road. It was adjacent to a hospital and had dozens of rows of gravestones that flowed up a gentle hill from the road. The site, rather unkempt with weeds and knee-high grass, was highlighted with flowers at the heads of gravestones.

"I hope everything works out for me," Bridget muttered, teary eyed, staring at the cemetery.

"It will," I replied. The thought of life without her, however, flickered through my mind for a brief moment. It was too much to bear.

We both worried about her most recent test results for inflammation. A couple weeks earlier, in her weakened neuropathic state from chemo, Bridget fell in a parking lot while carrying Andrew. He was okay, but Bridget injured her leg and upper left arm, the same side of her body where the cancer was located. El Hombre noticed an area in her injured location that, as he explained it, was "full." He said it could be inflammation from the fall or an infection. While he did not seem overly concerned, he had Bridget get a CT scan. The chemo was already shrinking Bridget's tumors, so it did not seem likely to the doctor that this "full" area would be a new tumor. Nonetheless, we were anxious about the results, which we would have upon our return home early the following week.

"I don't want to end up there," she said, referring to the cemetery.

"We all end up there," I said, "but you won't be there for a long, long time."

"I'm really scared. I can't stop thinking about it."

"Is Mom going somewhere?" asked Jack.

"Yes, she's going with us to the condo," I replied.

"What were you talking about?" asked Jack.

"Nothing."

For the first time as a father, I felt a debilitating sense of weakness and vulnerability in front of my kids. *What if we lose her?* I thought. As a kid, I had always looked up to my father. He had all the answers. He seemed invincible. Now I knew the fear and uncertainty he must have felt at times when he did not know what to do or where to turn for help. Yet somehow he had always created a sense of security for our family. He had put on the facade that things were just fine in the tough times, and now I was glad he had done so.

"Who wants some ice cream?" I asked, as upbeat as possible.

I felt like pulling off the road to vomit but plodded onward.

While I could sense Bridget was fatigued and the unknown test results stressed her, she did not show it in front of the kids. I felt energized not only by her resilience and will to be unaffected around Jack and Andrew, but also by her ability to handle her condition with such grace and dignity. She did not complain. Bridget would confide in me her feelings, not of fear, but of how the cancer was unfair to the kids, particularly if her condition were to deteriorate. It was never about her but always about how it affected others.

We enjoyed our ice cream on the crowded Branson promenade. It felt good to be around others. Most times I cringed at the sight of people in their normal healthy routines, without worry or care, but other moments it was comforting to be in their midst. There was a sense of security, and they were a distraction. A clown made the boys swords out of balloons, and they dueled against one another, swords in one hand and ice cream in the other. After their dueling, the ice cream was slathered all over their hands and faces, but it did not matter. They were happy, and thus so were we.

The high we had felt at Dogwood Canyon continued the next couple of days at the amusement park, at our condo's pool, and on a paddleboat on Table Rock Lake. After our last ride at the park, Jack looked at me, laughed and said, "Dad, I feel like I'm dead." I joined in his laughter, as I also felt spent, even nauseated from all of the park rides.

When Andrew awoke on the third morning of our trip, he muttered in his broken baby language that he wanted to go home. Jack concurred, so we packed and drove back to St. Louis.

I had been waking up before 5 A.M. each day of vacation, and I drove home bleary-eyed, coffee in hand. The uncertainty of Bridget's test results was on my mind, but at least I felt like the trip was a success. I reflected on our time together on the bike ride, at the amusement park, and on the promenade with gratitude. Even if things had been a struggle as of late, at least we had one another, as I noted in my journal:

Life is a mystery, magnanimous, electrifying, and terrifying all in one, but the greatest comfort of all is that we get to share this mystery, this wondrous journey, together. We are all in it together, thank God.

The boys watched a movie in the back while Bridget and I listened to our wedding CD. It was a compilation I had created for everybody who attended our wedding. We had not listened to it for a long time, and now, when we heard one of Bridget's favorite songs, "Forever and Ever Amen" by Randy Travis, it resonated with newfound meaning.

Travis sang, "Honey, I don't care, I ain't in love with your hair…if it all fell out I would love you anyway."

Bridget, beautiful and bald, glanced at me, held my hand, and smiled.

# MUSCLES AND MUSCLE CARS

\* \* \*

Prior to Bridget's diagnosis, we had contacted several con-
tractors for bids to paint our house. The estimates were
inconsistent at best and expensive. After learning about her
cancer and all of the impending medical bills, Bridget's brother Sean offered to do the job with the aid of friends and family.
We felt like a burden but accepted, and he organized a group
and planned to complete the entire project over Memorial Day
weekend.

I picked up the scaffolding from the hardware store in
Dave's old Chevy pick-up on Saturday morning. The truck was
more than twenty years old, red and rusted with creaky doors
and a busted radio and air-conditioner. Dave had kept the
truck just for this purpose—hauling whatever, whenever. He
kept it parked outside the barn at their house for the family
to use anytime. I made two trips to get the scaffolding, which
had many parts and was heavy, as I did not want to overload the
truck's suspension. Already I was sweating in the early hours
of an unusually warm and humid day in late May. I enjoyed
occasions such as these. Manual labor, driving the truck, and
working daylong and sweating was a good break from being
inside the office all week. It reminded me of the wilderness

adventure camp in Canada, when the days were long and the work was grueling yet satisfying.

We had plenty of muscle to help unload and assemble the scaffolding, including Sean, Bridget's cousin-in-law Ryan, and several others. Most of the painting on the first story had already been finished the day before by friends and family—a half dozen altogether. Now another half dozen chipped in to complete the project.

Two painted from atop the scaffolding, two worked from ladders, while two others were on smaller-scale scaffolding our friend Mike had brought in his own truck. A shop teacher at a public high school, Mike was the husband of one of Bridget's lifelong friends, Maggie. He was a handyman who enjoyed building decks in the summer for extra bucks. Mike towered over most with a lean and sturdy build, and his booming voice came in handy when he coached his school's football team.

"Your railing on the deck is looking rotted," he said from a ladder, analyzing the structure just above the front porch. It had become apparent, even from afar, that it needed attention.

"A little paint should do the trick, you think?"

"It needs to be rebuilt."

I paused, silent.

"Tell you what," Mike said. "If you get the wood, I'll rebuild it today."

A short time later, Mike knocked down the rotted railing from the deck with a sledgehammer, then measured the pieces carefully and cut the new wood from the bed of his truck, first with the circular saw for the straight vertical slats, then with the jigsaw to create the decorative curvature on the horizontal pieces near the top railing. His radio boomed with AC/DC, Led Zeppelin, and other classic rock legends. Somebody had brought a cooler of beer for the whole gang, and Mike casually sipped a cold Bud as he went to work on building the new railing for the porch deck.

Mike was a good conversationalist. He and I shared a passion for cars and camping. As I painted from the scaffolding at the front of the house, around the windows with a brush, then with the roller for the larger sections, we talked about the mountains and vistas and campgrounds in Colorado where he was taking a trip with Maggie and their kids that summer in his new ride—a camper he had just purchased for a bargain.

"It gets little more than a few miles per gallon," Mike chuckled. "Whatever we save on lodging we'll more than spend on gas."

Then we talked about our favorite muscle cars, his a '69 Camaro and mine a '70 Chevy Chevelle 454.

"If we had a drag race, I would just knock you off the road," I said. "That Chevelle is a tank."

In the midst of our discussion, I lost track of the pain in our lives and the monotony of the task at hand. I was overwhelmed by the generosity of others as I soaked in the scene, guys moving the scaffolding, filling up their buckets, slapping paint on the house and trading yarns all the while.

My escape from reality proved momentary, however, when Bridget opened the front door. Looking helpless, desperate, and in pain, she quietly motioned for me to come inside.

"I've never felt so bad," was all she could muster. The effects of chemotherapy were devastating her body.

I quickly got her some nausea medicine and a cold washcloth to put on her forehead as she rested in bed. It took some time for the medicine to go to work. Meanwhile, she lay moaning and quietly sobbing in pain. I sat in a chair next to the bed, the bright sun spilling through the window in sharp contrast to the dark dreary room, until the soothing effects of the medicine alleviated Bridget's pain to a more tolerable level and she slowly closed her eyes and went to sleep. I felt relieved for her and hoped the pain would subside, at least until the next round of chemo. Outside the music still rumbled and the crew continued painting as I remained beside Bridget, now snoring, and soon I became immobile in the soft recliner, my mind and body beat, exhausted, until my own eyes became heavy and closed.

When I awoke and went outside, the crew had all left. The deck above our porch was completely rebuilt and in place, already wearing a fresh coat of white paint.

After I returned the scaffolding, Bridget's uncle Mark brought over a truckload of ladders and painting equipment to finish the job. Mark and Dave set up ladders on the garage roof to reach the peaks of the second story. Sandy, Suzy, Sean, and our brother-in-law Don completed the trimwork, hanging out of windows to reach the last areas. Soon the twenty-year-old house was totally transformed.

Thanks to Sean and the efforts of friends and family, we had saved several thousand dollars by doing the project on our own. If I had married Bridget's whole family when I married her, as her brothers and cousins had jokingly contended, it sure had its perks.

# UNCLE PAUL

### * * *

Several months had passed since Bridget's diagnosis, and I realized I had yet to tell anybody about the visions I had had leading up to her diagnosis. While they did not worry me, I wanted to make sense of them and understand what they meant.

I knew I could confide in my friends and family, but I did not want to scare them. After all, my visions may have suggested a worst possible outcome, and if Bridget somehow learned about it, I knew it would exacerbate her fear and worry. I wrestled with the notion of telling the Jesuits. *Would they think I was insane? Would they think I was trying to get attention?* I was self-conscious about why I even had the visions to begin with, so I decided to wait. I would keep quiet so as not to spread any undue burden or stress on anybody else.

Ultimately, it was the Jesuits who came to see me. Shortly after Bridget's diagnosis, they offered to talk, and I obliged. I spoke with a couple of them separately in private and confided my feelings, thoughts, and visions. One of them, Father Marco, provided perhaps the most powerful advice I had ever been given.

"Do not ask God for His help," he told me. "He already knows. What you need to do is to thank God. Thank God every-day for what you do have, and you will become stronger."

While the advice helped tremendously, I was still confused by my visions, and I struggled with comprehending them until I met with my old friend and mentor Father Paul.

The president of a Jesuit high school in California, he was in town for a couple of days. Before moving west, Father Paul had served as president of the school where I now worked. Though he had moved around quite a bit earlier in his life, from New York and Boston to South Africa and Australia, he had come to know St. Louis as home.

Father Paul was older now yet still built solidly, with the raw grit and solid stature of a relief pitcher. In his heyday he played minor league baseball and could throw a football eighty yards. He could have been a professional athlete. For that matter, he could have excelled in the business world like his father, who at one time was a high-ranking executive of Pfizer Corporation. Father Paul was a born leader. He possessed a commanding presence, intimidating for those who did not know him well, and an ability to think strategically and set forth a vision for an organization. That said, Father Paul had abandoned any ambitions for worldly success in favor of a life entirely dedicated to helping others. He would come to measure his success not by accumulating wealth but instead by positively impacting the lives of others with unrelenting persistence and passion. He was truly a "man for others."

I had known Father Paul since sixth grade, when I attended his organization's wilderness camp for the first time, and had come to refer to him affectionately as "Uncle Paul." He was known for taking insane canoe trips that ventured into rough waters and rapids. I always admired that, so when I was old enough to lead the canoe trips myself, I did so with dogged determination to match or even top the scope and severity of his expeditions.

One time, I came to experience the challenge, thrill, and hell Father Paul must have endured on his own trips. At seventeen, I had the awesome responsibility of leading an expedition that ventured into the heart of the remote Canadian bush. I had been on several similar trips, yet none so demanding. My primary goal was to beat the record previously held by another expedition that had canoed the same distance—150 miles—in four nights. We would do it in half the time.

On the expansive network of crystal-clear Canadian lakes, winds would regularly whip the water into a foaming frenzy of white caps during the day. When fully loaded, each canoe weighed more than seven hundred pounds. Paddling with such weight into the unrelenting wind and waves was tough, and the slow progress was demoralizing. To compensate, I chose to begin our trip at 1 A.M. to make quick time across the water, which was typically calm and serene at night. I was able to navigate by the treeline, highlighted by the stars and moonlight and Northern Lights. When the sun rose, the winds would commence, and precious time and energy would be lost fighting the elements. The first day we paddled twenty hours.

After two days of canoeing for a total of nearly forty hours, we reached a portage and were greeted by a sprawling shoulder-high heap of deadfall left by a recent logging operation not on our map. Now, we would have to blaze our own pathway through the leviathan pile of bulky birch, pine, and maple with canoes and heavy supplies on our backs. Physically depleted and mentally exhausted, we began to unpack the canoes. It was high noon and uncharacteristically hot and humid for Ontario. Hundreds of miles away from the nearest town, it sounded like a freeway as the mosquitoes buzzed in huge swarms.

Carlos, the oldest staff member in our group, hurled his canoe onto his shoulders with impressive ease. He was of Philippine descent and endowed with prodigious strength, an easy-going attitude, and an uncanny sense of humor. The young campers followed him, carrying food, paddles, and other camping supplies.

I carried up the rear of the group to ensure that nobody and nothing was left behind.

Progress was slow, painfully slow, through the deadfall. Surgeon-like concentration was needed when stepping across the unsteady surface with the eighty-pound aluminum canoe on my shoulders while the mosquitoes feasted on my face.

About halfway through the three-mile trek of fallen trees, I saw Rick, the other staff member. He was in his late thirties, of medium height and build, with a short, military-style haircut. He had fair skin and was badly sunburned. Rick had hit the wall, both mentally and physically.

As I approached, he was vomiting.

"I used to be in the ROTC," he said, "and we had some tough training. But nothing like this. This is just plain insanity." He began to cry. "I can't take it anymore. I can't move on."

I sat with him for several minutes. The rest felt good, but we needed to continue. I heaved his Duluth pack, holding a tent and other supplies, onto my back, then threw the canoe onto my shoulders, and we plodded forward through the ravaged landscape.

The sun had just dipped below the horizon when all three of our canoes reached our final destination at the camp on the third day. Fatigued, famished, and all but broken, we paddled into camp singing. We had been to hell and back. Together, we emerged victorious.

The trip drew upon everything I had learned at the camp, including discipline, a need to be challenged, and love for God and others, the same values Father Paul had imparted to me through his example of compassion and leadership. Nothing good comes easy, I learned from my Jesuit mentor, and nothing easy builds character.

Following Bridget's diagnosis, I had felt like Rick on that canoe trip, completely spent and defeated, but I knew I must carry on. I knew Father Paul would push through the pain just as he had done on his own canoe trips. He would advance with mulish resolve, without complaint, and he would use his affliction as an opportunity to grow, become stronger, and make others around him better, more humble, and more grateful to God.

In addition to camp, some of my most significant life experiences could be linked, in some way, to Father Paul. He performed our wedding ceremony and helped arrange my semester abroad at the same Jesuit high school in Sydney, Australia, that he had attended as a boy.

I learned he was in town when the receptionist at school called and said, "Father Paul is here and wants to see you in fifteen minutes."

He expected promptness. I was at the switchboard in ten minutes.

When I saw him, he gave me a hug and patted my back with the impact of a linebacker.

"How are you?" he asked in his booming Boston accent.

As usual, he was only interested in hearing about others. He never spoke about himself unless he was asked, at which time he would humbly respond with a brief answer and quickly change the subject.

After we exchanged greetings, he said, "Let's talk in the chapel. I want to hear how Bridget is doing."

There were no students or teachers around in the summer, and the school's chapel was empty. We sat on some chairs near the back.

With some trepidation I told Father Paul about the visions.

He reflected briefly and said that God had been actively engaged with me and preparing me mentally for what was to come. My intuition was heightened before Bridget's diagnosis. He told me not to focus on what the visions meant in terms of Bridget's future, but rather to reflect on how they had prepared me for that moment in time.

"God has been strengthening you, comforting you," he said. "Continue to pray, and God will continue to be with you."

Preparation. God had been preparing me. It was such a simple yet ingenious and logical explanation. I had been so preoccupied with what the visions meant in terms of Bridget's condition that I had failed to understand that they were simply a means to help strengthen my faith, bring me closer to God and, ultimately, prepare me for what lay ahead.

This "preparation" seemed to have taken place well before the visions. I had made a pretty radical change in lifestyle about two years before Bridget's diagnosis. I had always wanted to complete a triathlon. Moreover, I had always had an all-or-nothing attitude when it came to setting and achieving goals, and almost overnight, I became bent on preparing for and achieving this feat. I ate healthier, put together a comprehensive training schedule, and exercised religiously. I became passionate about competing with others and myself, as I had as a youngster and throughout high school. There was a resurgence in my competitive nature, as well as my physical and mental well-being. I became stronger and more sharply focused than ever. I beat my personal goal for the triathlon and went on to pursue bike racing. On the surface, it seemed I had been preparing myself for a series of athletic competitions. But perhaps some greater force had been preparing me for a much larger, more challenging feat. At any rate, I felt God somehow had a hand in my mental, spiritual, and physical preparation, and I was thankful.

After our conversation, Father Paul said a prayer in Bridget's honor. When he prayed, he closed his eyes and spoke with emotion and intensity. As always, his words were unscripted, heartfelt, and flowed naturally.

Then, as quickly as he had come, Father Paul was off. He had another meeting. More lives to touch.

# THE BOYS AND BUDDHA

### * * *

S weat singed my eyes as I stood atop a ladder trimming tree branches in the front yard, one hand on the ladder and the other handling the chainsaw. It was oppressively hot with a heat index at 112. Jack came outside and said he wanted to go for a ride.

"Let's go forty or fifty miles," he said, climbing onto his bike to do a few warm-up laps around the circle.

"How 'bout four or five?"

"No, Dad, come on, seriously," he continued, genuinely disappointed.

In the coming months, he would continually refer to those forty or fifty miles he wanted to do, then it just became "forty fifty." He was an intelligent kid and knew how far "forty fifty" was, but his ambitions outstripped his three-year-old legs.

"Dad, you know I can ride my bike without hands?"

Bridget had told me on occasion he would ride without his hands. I knew he could do it, as he had total control and confidence, but I did not like it. For some reason, riding without hands put more fear in me than taking a downhill curve at forty-five miles per hour.

"Don't ever do that, Jack. It's dangerous."

"Oh, really," he said sarcastically.

"Dad, I'll ride without hands, too," Andrew chimed in.

"You'll be in the trailer, bud," I said, climbing down from the ladder.

Andrew was clad in only a T-shirt and a diaper. I had spent all morning doing yard work, so I was spent and too lazy to put any real clothes on him. Nobody would see him in the trailer anyway. He was intent on bringing his miniature Thomas the Train suitcase. It was animated and bright, a real attention-grabber, like a multi-colored, fluorescent zebra. He had a fascination with the thing for some reason, and it happened to fit snugly with him inside the bike trailer. He sat contentedly in the trailer, his head bobbing up and down, back and forth as we made our way along, diaper and suitcase and all.

As we rode, the heat pulsed off the pavement. Though I was never a fan of the stifling heat, I felt comfortable now as we pedaled on the sidewalks over the gentle rolling hills, navigating our way through the network of subdivision streets, in one neighborhood and on to the next, around cul-de-sacs and past the condominiums and swimming pool and tennis courts. Biking with the boys proved my greatest solace after Bridget's diagnosis. It gave Bridget a break and time to rest, it helped to clear my mind, and it gave the boys something to look forward to. Since her diagnosis, it was the boys who provided an invaluable source of strength. They also offered perspective, humor and, above all, companionship, as I noted in my journal:

> I'm totally content and relieved when I'm out doing something with the boys like hiking or bike riding. They put me at ease and I feel a little like R.P. McMurphy in *One Flew Over the Cuckoo's Nest*: rebellious, goofy, a bit loony, but mostly carefree. They have been such a blessing.

We passed a man walking his dog, and he said, "Look at that little rascal go. How old is he?"

"Three," I said.

"Well, I'll be," he said, shaking his head with a chuckle. "Just look at him go."

He was either supremely impressed with Jack's ability, or the man thought I was lying. Perhaps both.

Jack was persistent and undaunted when it came to riding. One evening earlier in the summer we had gone for a walk in the neighborhood. Jack was on his bike leading Bridget and me as I pushed Andrew in the stroller. He fell off his bike and badly skinned his knee. Blood poured down his leg, and he cried the entire way home. The following evening, though, he wanted to go riding with me. On the way down a sizable hill, I sped ahead to ensure he didn't run into the back of my bike. Just when I thought I was safely ahead, I turned around to see him, but he was nowhere in sight. As I turned my head back, I saw him right at my side. We were shoulder-to-shoulder, bearing down the hill at twenty miles per hour. The sidewalk was a mere few feet wide and provided no room for error. Jack looked up at me without flinching and grinned, then I gently applied the brakes and watched him sail down the rest of the hill on his own. I had known plenty of adult cyclists without his balance and confidence, and many more without his lack of fear.

On most rides we stayed in the subdivision. However, Jack knew that when I went for my "real" rides I would leave it, so he was always determined to do the same.

"Babies stay in the subdivision," Jack said while pedaling. "Come on, let's do a real ride."

"You guys want to go to the bridge?" I asked. The pedestrian bridge, a couple miles from our house, was over a busy thoroughfare along a jogging trail.

"Yes!" they exclaimed.

When we biked to the bridge, we would stay on the jogging trail and take a break near the shopping plaza, which included a grocery store, a bank, shops, and a couple of restaurants. Across the street was a small hotel and theater. There was an open grassy area with well-maintained landscaping and benches for resting, and soothing instrumental music played on small, inconspicuous outdoor speakers.

Andrew insisted on taking his Thomas the Train suitcase out of the trailer when it was time for our break. Passersby seemed both amused and perplexed.

The boys flanked me as we shared the water bottle. It was our favorite part of the ride. Today they had red Gatorade. They thought it made them look like pros.

As I sat transfixed in the moment, for some unknown reason Jack reached over and patted my belly and began laughing. Following suit as always, Andrew did the same, patting my tummy with a giggle. The boys were laughing hysterically, and soon I joined them.

"Do you think I have a big belly? You think I'm the Pillsbury Dough Boy? What, am I Buddha?" I asked, laughing uncontrollably. "Why are you doing this?"

"Because we just love you, Dad," Jack said.

Diaper-clad Andrew repeated parrot-like, "We love you, Daddy."

Cars still passed by, their drivers looking at us with the same curious and bewildered reaction as we continued sweating and drinking red Gatorade and laughing like mad idiots in the blazing hell of summer.

# RED DEVIL

**\* \* \***

Fireworks were rumbling and popping outside when I pulled Bridget from the bathtub and carried her to bed. Faint and pale, she was so limp that she felt nearly lifeless. Her legs were unable to support her weight, and she sobbed, exhausted. The poison had been assaulting her body for several months, and the cumulative effect had now become unbearable.

"I can't take it," Bridget spewed, naked, and utterly helpless. "I can't take it. I can't take it."

As I helped her into bed, a thunderous boom shook the house. The Fourth of July celebration outside was another dim reminder that the world was still rotating and rejoicing in its sparkling splendor despite our misery.

The day before, Bridget had received another powerful round of chemotherapy. It was a regimen that consisted of three toxic drugs—fluorouracil, epirubicin, and cyclophosphamide. The doctors called it FEC for short, though patients resentfully referred to it as the "red devil" because of its reddish hue and "evil" effects. It was the most punishing type of chemo, destructive to the cancer as well as the body. Typically Bridget did not feel the full impact of a chemo treatment until a couple days after, but the agony would last for a couple days then taper off into a more tolerable pain, nausea, and fatigue.

Though I had never experienced chemotherapy, I imagined it as a marathon hangover, which only had one cure: time. Similarly, I learned that the only way for Bridget to endure the pain of chemotherapy was also to will time away. Now, as she lay shivering in bed uncontrollably, it was clear she was no longer able to tolerate the pain or wait until the time passed. As I pulled the covers over her, I felt nearly as helpless as she.

"I can call the doctor," I said, "or take you to the hospital."

An earth-shaking bang rattled the windowpanes. It sounded like a war zone.

"I don't know," she replied, moaning like a poor helpless child. "I just don't know."

I placed a cool washcloth on her forehead.

"Let's see how you feel in a little while."

Times like this I envisioned Bridget's diagnosis as a shipwreck, and we were all floating in the rough sea totally exposed to the merciless sun and hungry sharks while struggling with an insatiable thirst. The boys had life jackets but were scared and needed attention, and Bridget was in pain, having endured a broken leg in the wreck, moaning and wailing in her own private hell, and I forgot about everything else for all that time, totally focused on keeping her calm and afloat and doing my best to stay positive and hopeful, never knowing what lay ahead or how much time we had left together. I had faith, but it was not easy. In survival mode, nothing else mattered but the singular focus of taking care of my poor lovely wife.

My heart sank as I stepped outside for some fresh air while Bridget rested. The humidity was stifling, but it felt good to be outside. Sandy and Dave had taken the boys to my aunt and uncle's house nearby to watch the fireworks. The fact that the boys were in good hands was the only ounce of reassurance. Watching Bridget endure this tore at me. Her suffering seemed inhumane, yet it was the only avenue for hope. I felt totally useless. Even the doctors had no formula, no magical pill to make the pain disappear. The Fourth of July, once a symbol of hope and freedom, now fizzled in my mind like a gigantic dud. The fireworks that occasionally appeared through the pines had lost their luster, and the festive pops and booms that once danced in the airwaves now rang in raucous discord. Nothing stung more than watching Bridget in pain, literally fighting for her life. She was my best friend, my partner in life, and a lifeline for our boys.

Something banged on the upstairs window.

I thought it was an errant bottle rocket, but the banging continued. There were no fireworks or anything making contact from the outside. Then I heard Bridget's voice, desperate, barely distinguishable over the explosions.

I bolted inside.

Upstairs, she was lying on the bathroom floor, surrounded by a pool of vomit.

The red devil was ravaging her body. It had robbed her of her appetite, leaving her severely dehydrated, malnourished, and nauseated.

Now she had reached her threshold and could not deal with the pain and nausea anymore.

"Let's go to the hospital," I said without hesitation.

"They can't do anything."

"We're about out of options, and they may be able to do something."

"Call Mary," she blurted. "Call Mary. Maybe she can help."

Mary was Bridget's nurse at the oncologist's office. Over the course of Bridget's treatments, the two had become good friends. In a field such as oncology, caregivers rarely befriended patients. After all, most cancer patients are destined for disappointment, pain, suffering, even death. From Mary's perspective, there was clearly more risk than reward at the onset of her relationship with Bridget. She had made a sacrifice, and Bridget was the grateful beneficiary.

The mood was emotional and tense when we met Mary at Bridget's first oncologist appointment. Before we saw the doctor, Bridget had pleaded to Mary, "I just want to live, I don't care what I have to do, I just want to live." Mary had been a consummate professional, saying all of the right things while simultaneously keeping her distance. However, as she absorbed more of the emotion, her mood began to change, and she became more distant, awkward, even short. She later confided to Bridget she was overcome with the intensity and emotion of the moment. She had never, in all her years as an oncology nurse, been so affected. Her life flashed before her when she first saw Bridget, who was sobbing, helpless, so plainly vulnerable. She could relate to Bridget because she also had children and was about the same age. She wanted to tell Bridget that she would live and everything would be okay, but as a professional she could not. That evening she drank a bottle of wine to cope with the stress and anxiety.

Bridget's friendship with Mary flourished with each chemo treatment. If another nurse attempted to tend to Bridget at the onset of one of her treatments, Mary would immediately intercede and take over. It was more than a territorial struggle. Mary was invested in Bridget's well-being, and Bridget was particularly relaxed and comfortable when Mary was taking care of her.

In the early summer, Mary invited her husband, Will, to meet Bridget at one of her treatments. Bridget brought new light and new life to the oncologist's office. Her smile and positive energy were infectious. Now Will was a fan of hers as well. Soon, our families met, first at a party at Sandy and Dave's house following the Komen Race for the Cure charity event downtown. Mary brought Will and their three kids. Later in the summer, we all celebrated Jack's birthday together at a pizza place.

Over time, the bond between Bridget and Mary became even stronger. Mary was always willing and available to support Bridget, both as a friend and as a caregiver. Bridget could pick up the phone at any time to talk as a friend or seek advice from a seasoned professional.

Now as I talked with her on the phone on the Fourth of July, Mary spoke calmly yet I could sense her anxiety. She reiterated the importance of keeping Bridget hydrated, even suggested taking her to the hospital for IV fluids.

"I'm sorry you have to be dealing with this," she told me. "It's just not right. Hang in there, and please call back if you need to."

Bridget insisted she lay in the bathroom until she felt better. She could not even muster the energy to be picked up. I put a pillow under her head and cleaned up the mess as she closed her eyes to rest.

The next day Bridget's condition had not improved. Sandy took her to the hospital while I was at work. Bridget's energy level and blood pressure were extremely low, enough that she had to lay down on the floor of the elevator at the hospital. There, in the elevator, she fell asleep. She only recalled waking up in a haze on a bed in the doctor's office, where she received IV fluids for several hours.

After Bridget recovered and regained some energy before her next round of chemotherapy, Mary confided in her with something startling. She said that she had to double- and triple-check the dosage levels of chemo she was administering to Bridget for each treatment because they were so high. The doctor knew her cancer was aggressive, and he was treating it accordingly. Also, Bridget was young, and her doctor knew that a younger, more resilient body could handle more punishment and recover more quickly than an older person's. He said he was hoping for a "grand slam," but it seemed he was trying to hit the ball out of the state.

# AUTUMN BLUES

\* \* \*

F all had always been my favorite part of the year, though I was now longing for a change in season after attending two funerals one day in September. Both of the deceased had succumbed to cancer. One was a student at my school, the other a dear family friend. I wanted to go to the funerals to show my support, but I knew it would be difficult and I was anything but prepared.

The first funeral was for Nick, who died at sixteen after battling cancer his entire life. The Mass was held at the church of a Jesuit university in the city. The neo-gothic church was stunning and impressive and more than 160 years old. A dozen Jesuits concelebrated the Mass, which was attended by more than one thousand, mostly students dressed in the school colors of blue and white to remember Nick's love for his school.

After Nick's death, one of our teachers said, "We needed Nick more than he needed us." The kid's peers and even his teachers were inspired by his unwavering optimism, his deep and mature sense of spirituality, and the courageous way he approached death. By the time he was nine months old, he had already undergone seven surgeries, five rounds of chemotherapy, and a bone marrow transplant. Over the course of his sixteen years, he had eighteen surgeries and consulted with more than twenty doctors. He lost a leg in one of the surgeries, but that did not stop Nick. He made the tennis team, helped manage the varsity football team, got his driver's license, and even traveled to Spain with his classmates, leaving two days after he found out his liver cancer had metastasized to his lungs. His mother said he referred to cancer as a blessing. When she asked what he meant, he told her, "Cancer is a blessing because it has made me who I am. It is all I know."

Father Marco, Nick's theology teacher, read a note from his mom after giving the eulogy. It was addressed to Nick. At the end of the note, his mom wrote that though he would no longer be with her, he was, at long last, home. She referred to him as her angel, and said the angels in heaven were happy that one of their own had finally returned. As Father Marco read the note, I thought about my own kids and their relationship with Bridget. I could not bear the thought of saying goodbye to either of them, ever. I began to feel lightheaded then to sweat. I wiped my eyes and looked at everyone else rubbing their own eyes.

I recalled the advice I had received from Father Marco about the power of gratitude, which was one of the hallmarks of Ignatian spirituality and had become my guiding light in times of dread and doubt. Instead of focusing on feelings of pity and desperation, I would be grateful for the incredible medical care Bridget had, for our huge support network of family and friends, and for our steadfast faith. Prayers of gratitude built me up more than those continually asking for something. As I sat amid the grieving flock in the church, I reflected on all the blessings God had bestowed on my family and me, even through Bridget's illness. These thoughts helped me to deal with the emotions, but I still could not bear to hear Nick's mother telling him goodbye.

On the way home, I met Bridget at the funeral parlor for the wake of Sue, a good friend of my mom's. I was a childhood friend of her son, Tom. Bridget had taken the news of Sue's death very hard. Sue had helped her cope with the shock and emotion after her diagnosis in the spring. She herself had been diagnosed a few years earlier with breast cancer, though hers was inflammatory, the type that spreads mercilessly and uncontrollably, with little hope for survival. The only option for most patients is to temporarily manage it.

Bridget developed a close bond with Sue. Cancer for them had become like a sisterhood. Sue took Bridget shopping for wigs and gave her several hats and scarves. She had a peacefulness that Bridget admired, and she stressed to Bridget the importance of faith and having a sense of humor in dealing with cancer.

Tom had been one of my best friends in grade school. He and I played soccer and spent several summers at camp in Canada together. In fact, Sue and my mom had shared a few summers at the camp with us as well. They were the cooks, and we were the campers. Tom and I were both avid fishermen, and we spent many hours together reeling in northern pike and smallmouth bass in Ontario. When we were back in St. Louis, we were catching perch and catfish at a nearby pond. After junior high, we lost touch. Our days of youth soccer were over, and we went to different schools. Throughout our childhood, Tom always seemed undefeatable. He was strong, tough, good looking with blond flowing hair, a standout athlete on the ice as a kid and then as a running back in high school. Growing up, Tom never wore a shirt. He liked to show off his physique. When we played soccer, he integrated the hip check from hockey into his game plan with ease and success.

When I saw him at the funeral home, for the first time Tom looked defeated. Though still in fine shape, he now had a solemnity about him, his head bowed as he spoke, his eyes bloodshot from crying. I had not seen Tom for more than fifteen years, though it did not seem nearly that long when we saw each other.

"Thanks for coming," he said, as we embraced in a bear hug. "It really means a lot."

We talked briefly, as there was a long line of friends and family behind us. After we paid our respects to Tom and his family, we left.

I drove home emotionally sapped and reflected on the lives of Nick and Sue and how, in many ways, they had become stronger through their own experiences with cancer. I especially admired them because, throughout their pain and suffering, they did not complain. Like Bridget, they were more concerned about others than themselves. Never had I more loathed—or been more cognizant of—complainers than after Bridget's diagnosis. I did my best to keep a positive attitude throughout her cancer, so when I heard others whine about the weather or carry on with petty gossip, I became despondent and feeling cynical. Thankfully, I did not let it harden me, but rather it made me appreciate even more how blessed I was to have Bridget, who had endured so much without broadcasting her every woe and worry to the world. I wrote in my journal:

There can be no greater testament to the resilience of humankind than the ability to overcome daunting odds with a smile and without complaint...and so Bridget transformed utter grit to glee with her effervescent spirit.

My admiration for Bridget grew as I saw the similarities between her and Sue and Nick. Her own faith let her realize that Jesus had endured the worst punishment and pain of all, and anything less was not worth complaining about. Bridget vowed to never use her cancer as an excuse for anything, but rather an opportunity to learn, grow, and strengthen her faith.

Maybe we did need Nick more than he needed us. Perhaps we needed both Nick and Sue more than they needed us.

Just after Bridget's diagnosis, Sue gave me a copy of a book written by the husband of a breast cancer survivor. The most powerful message in the book, more so than the author's words, was a note from Sue that she had stuck in the book. It read:

> Ben, I'm so sorry you have to go through this with your wonderful wife. God will bless you every day and you and her will get strength with the Holy Spirit and your faith. This book I hope will help you also.
> Love, Sue

Her note ended by saying she had taken solace in the Serenity Prayer, which she included:

> God grant me the serenity
> to accept the things I cannot change;
> the courage to change the things I can;
> and the wisdom to know the difference.
>
> Living one day at a time;
> Enjoying one moment at a time;
> Accepting hardship as a pathway to peace;
> Taking, as Jesus did, this sinful world
> as it is, not as I would have it;
> Trusting that You will make all things right

if I surrender to Your will;
So that I may be reasonably happy in this life
and supremely happy with You
Forever in the next.

*Amen.*

It was a simple yet powerful prayer, one that resonated with me. Sue had experienced the hardship, as well as the peace. She had once told Bridget of her love of butterflies. Sue said they were signs from God and that when one landed on your shoulder, it was a blessing from above.

I thought of how I needed a butterfly as I tried to put the day behind and, as the prayer said, take it one day at a time. I would even take "reasonably happy" for now.

# TROPHY WIFE

*** 

Amid the death around us, there was hope—hope that we found not only through our faith, family, and friends, but through Bridget's progress with her chemotherapy. The doctors had been tracking her closely, and as the chemo ramped up, her tumors were diminishing. In fact, they were nearly disintegrating. The pain and suffering, after all, seemed to be worth it.

We had known Bridget's treatment would consist of, sequentially, chemotherapy, surgery, and radiation. We did not know, however, whether she would undergo a lumpectomy or mastectomy—that is, partial or full breast removal, respectively. At the onset of her diagnosis, the doctors suggested the need to remove one or both breasts. Due to the overwhelming success of the chemotherapy, however, they left open the possibility of a lumpectomy. It was truly a best-case scenario, according to her oncologist, to be able to choose between surgeries.

Essentially, it became a personal preference between peace of mind and cosmetic appearance. Ironically, this decision was solidified with Bridget's excellent MRI results, which showed no trace of cancer. If the surgeon were to have done a lumpectomy, he would not have known what to remove without the tumor markers, as there were no longer any lumps. It would have been a guessing game with no guarantees. We did not want to risk Bridget re-experiencing her treatment regimen again, including chemo and radiation, if minute, undetectable traces should be left behind. After several doctor appointments, hours of research and talking with other survivors, we opted for a bilateral mastectomy, the removal of both breasts. I likened our options to those of a hunter, with the lumpectomy being a BB gun and the mastectomy a shotgun. The shotgun was the clear weapon of choice.

The week before her surgery, I threw a surprise party for Bridget. I had been planning it for several weeks to celebrate the successful completion of her chemotherapy. For a long time, we had not had anything to celebrate. Finally, we did.

Bridget was under the impression that a couple of our friends were coming over, but after they arrived, more continued piling into our house, friend after friend, many with gifts in hand, greeting Bridget with hugs and celebratory hoots and hollers.

My best friend from grade school, whom I had not seen in more than twenty years, flew in from Denver with his wife. Bruce had always been a big kid. We both went to grade school and played sports together. We were on the same swim team and competed with one another for first place at the meets. Before sixth grade, Bruce's family moved to Texas. Thereafter, we lost touch until college, when we talked over the phone one day for hours. Bruce liked to talk. He had grown to six-foot-eight and three hundred pounds, and had played football as a lineman for Arizona State and then Oklahoma until suffering a career-ending knee injury. We kept in touch infrequently after college, and after learning about Bridget's cancer, Bruce made an effort to keep connected with me, particularly through Bridget's CaringBridge site, where he was one of her biggest supporters with his colorful notes of encouragement.

When he arrived at our house, everybody turned to look at the big guy. Indeed, he had a large physical presence, but his presence was felt more in the way he carried himself. Bruce had a booming voice. He was jovial, positive, upbeat, and always cracking a joke.

One of Bridget's friends had a special cake made for the occasion. It consisted of two big boobs, side by side, each topped with pink-icing nipples, and the caption "Ta-Ta to Your Ta-Tas!"

When the cake was unveiled, everybody crowded around to take a look. Initially, they laughed and joked around. The laughter then turned to curiosity. *Who was going to eat the boobs?*

There had been so much food at the party that few people were still hungry. Yet the pink mounds sat there at the table conspicuously. When nobody took the initiative, Bruce stepped forward.

"What are you going to do with the cake, Bruce?" somebody asked.

Several others tempted Bruce. "Lick it," they said.

He grabbed the cake, minuscule compared to his gargantuan frame, and raised the sugary boobs near his face. Laughter erupted. Cameras flashed. Bruce's eyes grew large, his smile nearly as wide as the cake itself, then out came his tongue, which met the dark colored center of one of the mounds in a delicate, circular dance. When the laughter had reached a raucous crescendo, Bruce sank his face in-between the sweet mounds and shook his head rapidly back and forth like a dog trying to shake off water. People were crying with laughter as cameras continued flashing. The cake had served its purpose. It was an emblem of Bridget's belief in balancing the severity of her ordeal with openness and levity.

After the cake had been demolished, several of us, including Bruce, gathered around the fire pit in our backyard. It was good to talk with my old buddy as the fire cracked and sparked, and I felt blessed to have the support of so many friends, far and near.

The following week my wife said ta-ta to her ta-tas.

We were at the hospital the entire day for the surgery. I took Bridget to the hospital at 6 A.M. to prep and fill out paper work and listen to the nurses tell us about the risks and magnitude of the whole operation. She got emotional saying good-bye before being carted away. "I hope everything will be okay," she sobbed.

"I'll see you soon," I said, matter-of-factly. "It'll be all right, I know."

Her emotion somehow seemed to spill over into the waiting room, where her family and friends waited with me for hours. While I appreciated their support and care, it was difficult listening to and feeling their anxiety and fear and worry because I knew everything would turn out well. I hoped my confidence and sense of peace were not interpreted as uncaring or even naive, but I had absolute faith in her doctors and was certain of a positive outcome.

The mood in the hospital waiting room, nonetheless, wore on me. I felt lonely because I could normally rely on Bridget to be with me when I felt down, but now she was unconscious, on another level in the hospital, in another world as the surgeon did his handiwork, surgically removing her breasts and lymph nodes over the course of a few hours. I knew Bridget would be okay, yet the thought of being a single father occasionally slithered into my mind, and loneliness, which I feared so intensely, crept inward. I focused on prayer or something else, anything other than the empty forlorn feeling of being without Bridget. I killed time trying to catch up on sleep, to no avail, and then thumbing through magazines. Fifty years after the prime of one of my favorite authors, Jack Kerouac, one of his quotes coincidentally appeared in a copy of *Men's Journal:* "But let the mind beware, that though the flesh be bugged, the circumstances of existence are pretty glorious."

They were, indeed, glorious when Dr. K called Sandy, Dave, Bridget's siblings, and me into a conference room to report good news: The surgery had been successful, and Bridget was fine.

When I first saw her after operation, she said, "I'm so happy I did this." Even if it was the narcotics speaking, we felt blessed and at peace that we had made the best decision for us.

Bridget was uncomfortable and in pain following the surgery, her left side more excruciating where the lymph nodes had been removed. It was difficult for her to move, and she wore a tight white vest around her chest for the first week. Three plastic grenade-like drains hung from the vest and slowly filled with blood. I would empty them for her several times a day. The boys were fascinated by the drains, and Jack thought they resembled miniature footballs. He chuckled, "I wonder how far you could throw those things."

A few days after Bridget's surgery, Dr. K called with the pathology reports. It was the best possible news and outcome: There was no cancer anywhere. We were ecstatic.

The evening we learned this incredible news, Bridget and I drove to get some ice cream. My mom was staying at our house helping out for a week and was with the kids. Bridget asked me how I felt about all of her scars from the surgery. She sounded somewhat nervous and anxious, as if she did not expect an affirming response.

"It's a feather in your cap," I said. "Your scars are like a trophy on your wall."

She smiled.

"Heck, now I have a trophy wife."

She laughed, and we kissed.

# TO THE MOON AND BACK

* * *

Jack struggled with being away from Bridget when she was in the hospital after her surgery. He constantly worried about her. When she returned home, he would peer into our room at night with his big blue sorrowful eyes that would latch on to ours and not let go. The little guy was looking for answers. He was seeking consolation and continually requiring our presence. It reminded me of myself, helpless and despondent, the first week after Bridget's diagnosis.

One night when we were eating dinner, Jack said, "Mom, I'm just happy you're alive."

It was totally unprompted and out of the blue. Bridget and I were puzzled. She had been feeling emotional after her surgery, and Jack's comment had made her think, again, about the possibility of life for the kids without their mommy. I felt awful for her.

That night as I was giving the boys their baths, I casually asked Jack about what he had said during dinner.

"Did somebody tell you that you should be happy that your mom is still alive?"

"No."

"If nobody told you anything about that, I'm wondering why you said it."

"I was just saying it," he replied.

I used to say with sarcastic pride that Jack was "highly advanced." In my estimation, and in the eyes of others, he truly was advanced for his age in many regards. Not only was he physically gifted, he was, like many four-year-olds, very sensitive. But unlike most his age, he was introspective and had a gift for sensing things he had not been explicitly told by anybody. Indeed, he knew we were all happy to have his mommy still alive. He was not about to take her presence for granted.

Even before Bridget's cancer, Jack always seemed worried that his mom was going to leave him. He would worry about her if she was not in his sight. "Where is Mom?" or "When is Mom coming back?" he would ask. It was usually easy to alleviate his anxiety—Bridget would say "Mommy always comes back"—but we struggled with this notion after her cancer because we could no longer make the promise that she would not leave him.

Shortly after Bridget's surgery, she began radiation, and while it paled in comparison to the pain and agony of chemo and the bilateral mastectomy, it was hard on Jack. For six straight weeks, Bridget had to be at the hospital early in the morning of every weekday for radiation treatment. This posed a logistical challenge, particularly with child-care. On most days Bridget took Jack to a friend's house while she and Andrew went to the hospital. During her treatment, one of Bridget's best friends, Annie, came to sit with Andrew in the waiting room. The little guy did not mind it, and in fact he looked forward to the occasion because it meant getting spoiled with candy and treats and playing with Annie's iPhone. Conversely, the frequency of Bridget's visits to the hospital fueled Jack's anxiety. "Why does Mommy have to go the hospital everyday?" he would ask. "Is she going to be okay?" Cancer and all its complications and complexities were difficult to grasp for most anybody, let alone a burgeoning four-year-old brain.

Our family's hardship was clearly taking its toll on Jack. His worry and need to constantly be in view of Bridget intensified and became concerning. Jack's bedroom was across the hall from ours, and at nighttime he would edge himself to the end of his bed to look into our bedroom. He could only see me from his vantage, but if he sensed Bridget was not in our bedroom, he would walk over just to make sure she was there. Sometimes it would take him hours to go to sleep. Bridget and I were hoping it would be a phase he would outgrow, but over time his anxiety increased. One day while I was talking to my mom on the phone, I told her about Jack and became so emotional I could not speak. I felt bad for Jack and wished I could do something to make his worry go away. After stressing over the possibility of his anxiety becoming permanent, I spoke with a good friend who was a psychiatrist, and he suggested we take Jack to a therapist. When he said the only regret we would have was not getting Jack some counseling, I knew we had to do so. We decided to take him to an art therapist because he loved to draw and color. He was a budding Picasso and after the first session was already looking forward to the next. The counseling taught Jack coping mechanisms to deal with his anxiety, and after only a few sessions he gradually shed his worry. His anxiety would always be there to some extent, but it became more manageable and easier to deal with. He had a worry box, and when he had a worry he would write it on a piece of paper, fold it, and put it away in the small box. It seemed to work.

While Andrew was two years younger than Jack and unable to fully understand what was happening to his mom, he was affected nonetheless. After Bridget lost her hair and was no longer able to give Andrew butterfly kisses with her eyelashes, he was saddened.

"When are you going to give me a butterfly kiss?" he would ask.

She would respond by giving him an Eskimo kiss, rubbing her nose against his. He did not externalize his emotions like his older brother, but his sadness could be felt. He just wanted things to be the way they were.

While the emotion of the boys at times took its toll on Bridget and me, it also helped us survive. Jack and Andrew were like everybody else in that they simply loved Bridget and wanted her to live, and they wanted their feelings to be understood. Moreover, their innocence and humor helped us to keep things in perspective. When they saw the ink markings the doctors had made on her chest for radiation, they responded by saying, "You're not supposed to color on people but on paper." At times, Jack and Andrew would wear Bridget's wigs around the house acting like goofballs, playing with her prosthetic boobs and tossing them around the room like they were mini Nerf footballs.

When I tucked in the boys for bed, I would read them a Bible story, and then I would let them talk about their day. They would run through the whole litany of when they awoke, what they ate, what they did, who they played with, and on and on. Then they would ask me a simple question that would turn into a fifteen-minute discussion.

"What is space?" Andrew asked once.

They had asked about space before when Bridget told them she loved them to the moon and back. They asked where the moon was, and we predictably replied that it was in space. But the question of what space was seemed trickier to answer. I had several illustrated books about space, and we thumbed through one about the solar system, each page leading to more intrigue, amazement and, ultimately, more questions.

"How old is the solar system?" Jack asked.

"Four-point-nine billion years," I replied.

"What is the solar system?"

"It's a group of eight planets with the sun in the middle of it," I said, referring to a colorful diagram. "It used to be nine planets when Dad was your age, but since then a bunch of scientists decided Pluto should no longer be considered a planet, so it's eight."

"What does the solar system do?"

"The planets all go in the same direction around the sun, and—"

"But what is outer space?" Andrew interrupted.

When I felt we had concluded our discussion on space and it was time for bed, they wanted to hear more.

"I'll tell you more tomorrow night," I said.

"Tomorrow night we want to know about all of the rules of football," Jack said.

"All of the rules," the little one chimed in. "Every one of them."

# PART THREE

# MAGIS

\* \* \*

In early January, I flew to Orlando to meet up with Bridget and the boys, who had arrived days earlier to visit her brother Brian. Our trip to Disney World had been postponed nearly one year, but we were finally going. We would be there as one big happy family, finally, like all those families at the egg hunt last Easter that had nauseated me in the midst of my despair.

At long last, our former lives seemed to be resurrecting themselves, slowly, surely, miraculously. However, I felt restless. I wanted to do more than simply be a good father and supportive husband. Somehow I wanted to manifest the compelling inner strength that I had experienced over the past year, beginning with the visions and Isaac's talk and culminating with my newfound perspective and spiritual transformation.

As a copywriter in advertising, I had always been taught to ask one simple question when trying to sell a product: SO WHAT? Sure, you may have a great product, but SO WHAT? Now I was asking myself the same question. We had come a long way as a family, and all things considered I felt I had done a fairly good job of holding things together as the so-called head of the household. But I wondered if that was enough. *So what?* I thought. *Is that good enough? Is that it?* I thought about a word often used by St. Ignatius—*magis*, meaning "more" in

Latin. He urged others to seek the *magis* by constantly striving to go further and do "more" for the greater glory of God. To some degree, I had done "more" for my family in the past year than I ever thought possible. But what would I do in the future for them, others, and God? How could I transform the immeasurable strength I felt into something tangible, something helpful to others?

No matter how hard I tried, I could not fall asleep on the flight to Orlando, rotating from closing my eyes to peering out the window at the infinitesimal lights of small towns sporadically gliding past miles below. It was quiet inside the cabin, but outside, in the upper reaches of the stratosphere, the plane battled the frigid elements, hurtling through the jet stream. I tried to relax to some instrumental music on my iPod, though it did little to soothe my nerves, which were in turmoil like the pounding wind outside.

An intense feeling of gratitude overwhelmed me as I reflected on the fact that Bridget's life had been saved by a drug that had just recently been approved by the FDA. Herceptin had been developed by Dr. Dennis Slamon, a research doctor at UCLA, a man deeply passionate about ending cancer. I could not cure cancer, but I could ride a bike. I thought there might be a way to fuse my passion for riding with raising awareness for cancer and support for the cause. After all, Dr. Slamon's success would have never been possible without the help of many generous donors. My mind instantly ignited and began racing. I wanted to do something big, really big. I continually thought about two words: simplicity and magnitude. *Keep it simple, but make it big,* I thought. I then reflected on my post-college days when I used to ride on the Katy Trail—the former Missouri-Kansas-Texas Railroad that had been converted to a bike path and stretched across Missouri. I could bike the whole damn thing. I was sure others had done it, but how many had done the entire trail in one day?

Over the next several days, I could not shake the idea. The more I thought about it, the more it made sense. It was simple, had tremendous magnitude, and would be for a good cause. The feat would be well suited for my long gangly legs, which excelled on endurance rides but never had the power to produce the short, violent bursts of speed needed to win criterium races. Moreover, it was a unique, monumental cycling challenge that did not involve racing, so it would put Bridget's mind at ease. Since my accident, she was not too keen on the idea of my racing again, so I had agreed to focus on time trial events, which would essentially eliminate the possibility of another accident. The time trial, of course, is the ultimate "test of truth," and I was excited about the challenge. It was something new, another form of cycling. The ride across the state, in a sense, would be a time trial event elevated to a new plateau. I had always wished it had been me, not Bridget, to have cancer. I hated to see her endure the pain. Now it would be my turn to feel some of the pain, albeit a fraction of what she underwent.

I had come up with some far-fetched ideas throughout my marriage, ideas that were typically greeted with sarcastic head-nodding and rolling eyes, so I introduced the concept gradually. I told Bridget I was considering riding halfway across the state on the Katy Trail as a fundraiser. While she did not shoot down the idea, she did nod her head and roll her eyes. Several times I wanted to talk about the idea, but she kindly changed the subject.

I had never been to Disney World and had never been eager to go, but we all had a good time at the park and enjoyed Sea World, too. The weather allowed us to hit the beach. Andrew loved the "sandbox" as he called it, and it was nearly impossible to drag Jack out of the water. We always knew our boys were pretty low maintenance, but when they told us the beach was their favorite part of the trip, even better than Disney, we were tickled with joy. We relished knowing that they could enjoy the simpler things in life at such a young age, and that they would not be begging us to go to Disney and spend a small fortune every year. More refreshing was watching Thunderbird and Sharp Arrow play together like best friends. Their personalities were blossoming and so was their relationship as "best buddies," as they affectionately referred to each other.

Bridget and I went to see Cirque Du Soleil on our last night in Orlando while the boys stayed with Brian and his wife Corrina. Before the show, we strolled the promenade of Downtown Disney and visited a cafe, where I consumed several chocolates, one espresso, and a hot fudge sundae. During the show I shared some of Bridget's soda. All the caffeine kept me up nearly the entire night after we returned to her brother's house, thinking about the incredible talents and eccentricities of the Cirque Du Soleil performers and the risks they took, all for the sake of entertainment. One of them had climbed a stack of tables and chairs that teetered and swayed more than thirty feet in the air, then casually did a handstand with one hand while waving to the audience with the other. Inevitably, however, my caffeinated mind returned to the idea of the bike ride, and how I might use my own talents for an even greater purpose.

At breakfast, before we left, I threw the whole concept out there for everybody to gnaw on. Bridget's brother and I had been talking about cycling, a passion we both shared.

"You doing any triathlons or races this summer?" Brian asked.

"I'm going to do a long ride to help raise money for Bridget's Komen team," I said to Brian and Corrina as Bridget listened nearby.

We supported the charity Susan G. Komen because it had provided Bridget much-needed support after her diagnosis. Komen connected her with other survivors, who offered advice, hope, and a positive outlook. It also raised breast cancer awareness and funded more research for the disease than any other organization in the world. She sponsored a team that raised money for the charity by participating in the Komen Race for the Cure, a popular walk/run event.

"Wow, that's great," they both said unison.

"I'm going to do the whole Katy Trail in one day."

Bridget, who had wanted some normalcy in our lives for once and was not ready for any big adventure, promptly replied, "He means half the trail in a day."

"The entire trail," I said.

"What?"

"How far is that?" asked Brian, enthralled by the idea.

"It stretches across the state," I told them. "More than two hundred miles."

Bridget smiled and nodded and said that was great, then quickly changed the subject.

# KATY TRAIL

*  *  *

Back when Todd and I worked together, the head of our ad agency hosted a company party at a winery in Augusta, a quaint village on the bluffs overlooking the Missouri River valley thirty miles west of St. Louis. About six miles outside Augusta, he rented bikes for everybody to ride to the winery on the Katy Trail. Our group started in a gigantic cluster that maneuvered snail-like along the trail. It was a party, not a race, but my claustrophobia and competitive nature quickly drove me to the front, followed by Todd and another co-worker, Jessica. Soon the trail opened up like a pebbly neverending ribbon unrolling into the horizon.

We had been biking for more than an hour when we realized that we should have already reached the winery. I had been keeping a good pace, and Todd and Jessica were following closely.

"Ben, do you think we missed Augusta?" Todd asked.

"It's got to be up ahead," I said. "Let's keep rolling."

"This is crazy," Jessica said. "There's no way it's this far."

Nobody else was anywhere in sight, nor had they been for some time.

By now our rears were getting sore, and we had depleted our water bottles. The sun baked our skin, and heat and humidity radiated oven-like from the gravel path, but we continued to ride. Aside from the fatigue and distress knowing that the others would think we were lost, it was an adventure, and I did not want it to end.

"Forget the winery, let's ride to Columbia," I joked. Columbia was a college town about sixty miles west.

After more than an hour of riding, we decided to turn around. I did so begrudgingly.

It was my first taste of the Katy Trail, and I was hooked. The nation's longest rails-to-trails project, the trail ran across the state and meandered peacefully along the Missouri River in the midst of rugged farmland and old-school Americana. Vast fields with rich soil and roaming livestock sprawled for miles on either side of the river. More than half of the 225-mile trail followed Lewis and Clark's path up the Missouri River, where river bluffs towered above and eagles circled overhead. Situated in an idyllic setting, the trail was relaxing. The mind could think, rest, and reflect there. From a biker's perspective, the trail was ideal, isolated from traffic aside from the few road crossings. The trail was covered with crushed limestone, which offered far more rolling resistance than asphalt or concrete.

After our work party at the winery, I would regularly drive to the trail with my bike for long weekend rides. I would take my old hunk of steel with fat tires, throw on a backpack with some water and food, and head onward with my headphones, dialed in to my own thoughts, totally at peace. I was typically garbed in tennis shoes and shorts with my shirt wrapped turban-like around my head. I was not bent on making time or miles, just focused on getting some exercise and reenergizing my soul away from the noise of the city and the stress of work. On those reflective days of riding, I got to know the rhythm of the trail, its charm, beauty, and its idiosyncrasies.

I learned how to ride the trail and keep a steady pace despite the wind, which would gather momentum on the open fields and across the river and push me back or throw me from side to side. The flat, unassuming nature of the trail was deceptive. It looked easy, but the bike could not coast due to the rolling resistance of the trail surface. There were no downhills, so there were no breaks unless you got off your bike or had the rare pleasure of a swift tail wind. Constant pedaling was the only way to make one's way on the trail. Over long hauls, the mental challenge of the monotony could exceed the physical demands associated with the nonstop pedaling.

The easternmost edge of the trail was in St. Charles, just outside St. Louis, and the western end of the trail in Clinton, southeast of Kansas City. Between these endpoints were twenty-six trailheads and two fully restored depots. The state capital, Jefferson City, was the largest city along the trail, and at about the halfway point. Most of the trailheads were in small farm towns that were once thriving communities along the rail line.

Hermann, near the McKittrick trailhead about sixty miles west of St. Charles, was the town along the trail with the most character and heritage. Established in 1837, the picturesque German settlement boasted historic architecture, award-winning wineries, bed and breakfasts, and short, steep hills that offered breathtaking views of the river and surrounding valley. Hermann had Old World charm. It was the center of the state's wine industry and a favorite destination of Missourians. Before Jack was born, Bridget and I would go to Hermann's Octoberfest, joining thousands of others to take in brilliant fall colors, oom-pah bands, brats on the grill, and ever-flowing wine and beer.

Hermann was about a ninety-minute drive from our house. Never had I imagined biking that distance, let alone the entire Katy Trail.

If I were to take on such a challenge, however, I knew I could do it on a bike. Over time, cycling had become more than merely a physical exploit. On one ride during college, I lost myself in the serpentine switchbacks of Virginia, a scenic circuit of enchanting Blue Ridge country roads garbed only in an undershirt and cut-off denim shorts. I saw a turkey, a bald eagle, verdant mountains, budding fields, a rolling mile-long freight train, old tractors, rusted-out cars, and dilapidated barns while biking thirty miles to the New River where I took a dip in the shallow crystal shoals and shouted at the surrounding mountains with glee and shock from the spring-fed water. The ride back was mostly uphill, and the pedals began to tear into my bare feet as I struggled to stay upright. My roommates nearly committed me to an institution when I returned beat-red and with my shirt wrapped around my head like a turban. I had been riding for five hours. *Look at what you missed!* I thought, as they resumed watching television, exactly as they had been when I left. I'd always longed to annihilate the staid, timid state of contentment and, in a way cycling achieved this by seeking adventure and awakening my inner being.

As I looked ahead, I realized I would be confronting something far more daunting than complacency or contentment—an end to cancer.

# KING TUTTS

*** 

King Tutts frequented the penalty box as a standout hockey player in high school. Though I did not know him at the time, I often saw him when I worked as a scorekeeper as a part-time gig. Aside from keeping track of shots on goal, I was responsible for recording the names of players who scored and those who earned penalties. When his team played, I scrawled his name under both categories several times per game. His foul mouth matched his outstanding play when he was penalized, cursing the referees with brazen intensity. Some referred to him as Racki—the talented goon who always held a grudge on the ice in the hockey classic *Youngblood*—for his fiery attitude, but I called him by his last name, Tuttle, which evolved into simply Tutts and then King Tutts. As the scorekeeper, I was inevitably put in an awkward situation when irate players visited the penalty box, which was in my area. They were like prisoners who had done no wrong, and as part of their verbal sparring they all claimed they had been with the referee's mom the night before.

Tutts was a teammate and longtime friend of Bridget's brothers and cousins. Together, they were the stars and enforcers of their team. After meeting Bridget, I became acquainted with Tutts at various social events. When I first met him, I was surprised at his civility. His on-ice scowl had been replaced by a permanent smile, and his intensity had transformed to a cool, laid-back nature. I had always been a tad leery of those who talked incessantly, and King Tutts liked to talk, albeit with less sound and fury than in his days as a hockey stud. As time went on, though, I got to know him well and learned that his gregariousness was no façade. He was a sincere, spirited conversationalist genuinely interested in others. Down-to-earth and not concerned about what people thought of him, he would tell you how he felt about anything. With Tutts, what you saw was what you got.

Soon after I got into biking, Bridget's brother Brian and her cousin Josh purchased road bikes, and in due time Tutts did the same. We all lived near each other and went for rides together early on weekend mornings.

When I thought about biking the entire Katy Trail, I knew I had to do it with somebody else. The drafting support of another rider would be just as critical as the mental and emotional support over the course of a ride that would take at least fourteen hours, the record held by a former professional at the time. Only a few cyclists had ever completed the feat of riding the entire trail in one day. Tutts came to mind as a riding partner because of his natural athletic prowess and innate competitiveness. Above all, like me, he was a dreamer.

I called him when I returned from Florida to tell him about my plan. "We need to meet somewhere this week," I told him. "I've got an idea for a ride. It's gonna be big."

"What is it?" He insisted I tell him about it before we met. "Hell yeah," was his response. "When are we gonna do it?"

We needed a plan, so we met at a bar for our first official planning meeting. It was also my last drink of alcohol for the next four months, which I dedicated to training for the ride. Tutts brought a book about endurance cycling and was revved up about the whole concept.

"This is awesome, dude," he said over and over. "What a great idea."

When the waitress delivered one of our drinks, Tutts asked her, "You know about the Katy Trail?"

"Yeah."

"We're doing the whole thing in one day for a fundraiser," he said, giddy.

"How far is that?"

"It's two hundred twenty-five miles."

"No way. That's crazy."

"What, don't you think we can do it? C'mon, look at us." There was a pause. "So you think we're nuts?"

"Yes."

Neither one of us had ever ridden more than seventy miles in one day, so we knew we had to put a plan together quickly and start training. Tuttle's enthusiasm and encouragement were refreshing. I knew some would think I was crazy for considering such a feat, but at least with Tutts' support, they would think we were both nuts.

# FIRST CENTURY

### ✳ ✳ ✳

A mix of freezing rain and snow assaulted my car, the wipers providing little help as the ice thickened on my windshield. I had to occasionally roll down the window and stick my head out to navigate the dark roads leading west to the Katy Trail. The forecast had called for unseasonable weather on this early spring day. I told Tutts and Josh it would be a game-time decision, and at 4:30 A.M. I texted them: "Let's roll."

We arrived at Weldon Spring, a trailhead near St. Charles, before 6 A.M. It was still dark, though lightening slowly and gloomily. The trail was covered in a thin blanket of wet snow.

"This is crazy," they both muttered numerous times. "You could have picked a better day to do our first century ride ever."

Josh was not planning on biking the entire Katy Trail with us, but had agreed to join us for our first hundred-mile ride. Like Tutts, Josh was naturally athletic, though thinner, and was an excellent hockey player in high school.

If Tuttle and I were to bike the entire Katy Trail in one day, we would have to ride at least three centuries beforehand to prepare our bodies, physically and psychologically. I rigidly adhered to the training schedule, which included two centuries and one 150-miler. I knew that if we could stick to the plan we would be successful.

Tutts lightened the mood with his usual chatter as we set off, but after only ten miles he had to stop to put some warmers in his shoes. The cold was tolerable, but coupled with the wet, windy conditions, it was already taking its toll and slowing us down.

The trail had a rolling resistance factor of about twenty percent, meaning it was that much harder to pedal than pavement. This factor increased when the trail became wet. A few weeks earlier, I had ridden sixty miles from Hermann to St. Charles. Though it was a dry day, it had rained for two days before, and the trail had become intolerably slow. Because the trail was maintained differently in various sections, some parts were slower than others, and on the particularly slow parts my thin road tires would sink into the soft wet trail. I had planned on averaging seventeen miles per hour—equivalent to more than twenty miles per hour on pavement—but the boggy trail had slowed my overall pace to sixteen miles per hour. I had started the day fresh and confident but finished demoralized and spouting profanities.

It was much the same with Tutts and Josh. Fighting the elements, we dealt with the distractions nature threw our way the best we could. We had hoped to finish the century in six hours, but given the trail's increased rolling resistance and the horrid conditions, I knew it could be closer to seven hours. I was intent on finishing as soon as possible to end the agony and to alleviate any worry on Bridget's part. Cell phone service was unavailable on much of the trail, so I was unlikely to call her with status updates. I kept a steady pace and pushed onward, Tutts and Josh following behind as time progressed.

We took a break when we reached the halfway point near Hermann, where we would simply turn around and head back to Weldon Spring. By now it was light outside, though still cloudy, and the snow and freezing rain had turned to a light drizzle. We sat beneath the trailhead shelter on a bench, inhaling our energy bars and gels and refilling our bottles and CamelBaks with water from the fountain. We looked at each other, near disbelief, cold, tired, our bodies aching, realizing there was only one way home—to ride another fifty miles back. Once I had consumed my food and refilled on water, I threw on my CamelBak and got on my bike.

"You guys ready?" I asked.

"I need some more time," Tutts said. "I'm not in a rush."

Josh agreed.

Neither of them had kids, and I felt guilty leaving Bridget with the boys for the better part of the day. In addition, I needed to return by midafternoon so we could go to Mass.

"I need to try and make some time and get back soon," I said.

They were not budging. Somewhat reluctantly, I set off on my own, realizing they had ample supplies and would be fine. Though I did feel a little guilty, I was eager for the challenge of finishing the ride on my own.

The monotony and mental and physical agony peaked at about seventy-five miles, when each mile seemed to pass slower than the last, and my legs burned and began to lock and stiffen with each pedal stroke. There was no reprieve from the elements, which nearly brought me to a standstill on one wide-open section, the wind and cold drizzle battering me from the front and the sluggish trail tugging at my tires. When I reached Weldon Spring, I nearly collapsed. It had not been pretty, but the trip mileage on my bike computer read 100.00 for the first time ever, and I knew with the added rolling resistance it was equivalent to more than 120 miles in normal conditions on pavement.

After Tutts and Josh completed the ride, they called me.

"That was totally nuts," Tutts said. That was about all he could say.

That was all I could say as well.

I had made my decision to ride in the morning before even looking outside. Nothing short of a blizzard would have stopped me. I was set on riding the entire trail in one day, and aside from confidence, the only path to attaining that goal was disciplined training.

I had spent some time putting together a training plan and was faithfully adhering to it. Six or seven days a week I was on the bike. During the week, I would jump on the trainer for at least an hour at night after the boys had gone to bed. It was somewhat less than ideal, getting my heart revved up and eating the fourth meal of my day just before bedtime, but it was better than waking up at 5 A.M. or earlier. On the weekends, I would ride early in the morning to avoid traffic and to be able to spend the rest of the day with Bridget and the boys.

With each ride, my confidence was building along with my strength and endurance. I watched one of my favorite movies, *Breaking Away,* a few times for added motivation and inspiration, and like the "cutter" Dave Stoller who imitated the famed Italian cyclists, I started shaving my legs. Bridget enjoyed ribbing me about this, and I quickly developed a new appreciation for the cosmetic regimens of women.

# PAY IT FORWARD

* * *

O ver the next couple of months, I completed two more century rides, both on the Katy Trail, to ensure I was fully adapted to the riding conditions for the 225-miler. The first I finished on my own, achieving my goal in under six hours, equivalent to well under five hours on pavement. Tutts and I planned on riding 150 miles for our final training event.

His wife Laura drove us two hours west to Boonville, where we began pedaling east in the morning, headed for St. Charles. Tutts hit the wall after about fifty miles, then sluggishly followed my lead for another fifty miles to Hermann. He had not been properly refueling his body, so we decided to end the ride early after a hundred miles and hitch a ride home. Near Hermann it began to rain, and when we arrived in the small town it had become a pelting downpour. Just twenty feet from the tavern where we planned to take shelter, Tutts got a flat tire. The tire exploded like a shotgun. It had been that kind of day, and though Tutts was terribly apologetic about being unable to complete 150 miles, I felt relieved that the major training components were behind. Above all, I felt ready for the big ride just a few weeks later.

In addition to the training, all other preparations for the ride were coming together. My dad had agreed to be my support crew for the entire day, a role that entailed meeting me at each trailhead and refueling me with food and water. He was flying in from Virginia to assist. Bridget had helped to create some buzz for the ride, and several media outlets were interested in doing stories, which fueled our fundraising effort. We had set a goal of raising ten thousand dollars for Bridget's Brigade, her team for the Komen Race for the Cure. The team had raised about five thousand dollars the previous year. We hoped to double that amount, and, just a few weeks before my ride, we had already achieved this goal.

At home, things were looking up. Bridget was nearing completion of her Herceptin treatments and thus the end of her medical fight against cancer. She had visited the hospital on at least a weekly basis for more than fourteen months, but the end was finally in sight. We were anxious to put the brunt of the difficult experience behind us, particularly for the sake of our boys. They were constantly hearing people asking how Bridget was doing, and while the questions were always well intended, they were a reminder, another reinforcement that cancer was still at the center of our lives.

Several weeks before her last Herceptin treatment, Bridget began experiencing headaches, dizziness, and back pain. The old fear and doubt crept back into our minds. She reluctantly told her oncologist about the pains, knowing it would result in another dreaded round of tests. The anticipation and fear of the unknown carved her innards for days before the tests, and she cried throughout them and worried for two days about the results. Watching her suffer was excruciating, nearly as difficult as it was to digest the news when we first learned of her diagnosis. Our misery turned to glee when the doctor called to say the results were clear, and we thanked God for giving us yet another chance, another opportunity to experience the miracle of life with our boys.

Our celebratory spirit was bittersweet, however, as Bridget learned just after her good results that her friend Lori, whom she had met through her oncologist, had received negative news from her PET scan, a test commonly used on cancer patients to detect tumors through the use of radiation, or nuclear medicine imaging. Bridget and Lori were the same age, and both had two young kids. Spots had appeared on Lori's hip and spine. It was devastating news. Learning of her results was a grim reminder of my mom's friend Sue, who had had the same type of cancer as Lori—inflammatory, stage IV.

In the midst of the emotional ups and downs, Bridget had a sort of revelation in talking with another HER2-positive breast cancer survivor she met. Bridget told her that she was excited to talk to her because she had only met one other HER2-positive survivor. The woman responded by saying that there were only a handful of HER2-positive survivors because Herceptin, the main hope for those afflicted with HER2-positive, was so new. This comment gave Bridget a new perspective on how blessed she was to be the beneficiary of amazing medical advances.

It also provided us with renewed vigor to live by our faith, not by the circumstances of our lives, and to try to do some good for others. After all, it was because of the generosity of others who had supported charities and funded research years ago that Herceptin had been discovered. Now it was our turn to pay it forward.

# REDEMPTION

*  *  *

I awoke at midnight to the whistling of wind and pelting of hail. The flash of lightning pulsated like a strobe light through the hotel curtains, the rumbling continually shaking our room. We had seen the gigantic storm that covered several states on the weather forecast several hours earlier. It had been moving toward Clinton and to the northeast, the same direction I would be headed. Now that it had reached us, it would not soon go away. I had planned on doing the ride a few days earlier, but was forced to postpone it due to heavy rains and tornado warnings. Now the weather was no better. It was already the wettest spring on record, and the weather had further deteriorated.

I would have two enemies to engage—the distance and, now, the storm. Moreover, I would have to do it all alone. Tutts' confidence had been shot during training, and because of a scheduling conflict with his work, he was unable to ride the entire trail with me. He hoped to join me near the end.

I could not distinguish between dream and reality as I tossed and turned in bed, thinking of the rain and wind and hail. At about 3 A.M., the clash of thunder mixed with the hailstorm and woke me for the day.

I stumbled out of bed before the alarm clock sounded at 4 A.M. The restless night had charged my body with adrenaline. I felt like I had gulped several cups of coffee.

The night before I had lined up my riding gear, including a pink breast cancer wristband, on the hotel dresser. Until then, I had never worn it. I wanted to save it for the big ride. The thunder rattled the room and the rain continued to batter the window, but it did not matter. As I slid the wristband on, I knew I was going, regardless of the wet fury outside.

"What do you think?" my dad asked as we finished packing. He had a pale look of dread, doubt, and concern.

"It's raining pretty good out there," I said, evading the crux of his question.

"Are you really going to do it?" he asked, as a thunderbolt jolted the hotel.

"Let's roll," was all I said.

As we passed through the lobby with our gear and the bike, an old man working at the front desk suddenly seemed to awaken. He tilted his head down so he could peer over his spectacles situated low on his nose.

"You really going to do it?" he asked. The previous evening we had told the receptionist about the ride, so word must have spread.

"Yep," I said.

"Well, good luck," he said, shaking his head.

The day before, we had visited the Clinton trailhead demarking the western end of the Katy Trail so we would be familiar with how to get there in the morning darkness. Though it was only a few miles from the hotel, we struggled to find our way through the dark and unrelenting rain, the gargantuan puddles pulling our car from one side to the other as we tried to navigate through town. About fifteen minutes later, we arrived.

We sought shelter under the trailhead canopy. As I made final preparations, my dad scrambled to turn on the video camera, a loaner from a television station to capture b-roll footage. We were both unfamiliar with how to use it, and as we tried hopelessly to set it to record, our flashlight seemed to drown in the pitch black. There would be no official farewell, which was fine with me, as I was rather awkward on camera. It was also a small moral defeat, though, as I knew we could have figured it out in calmer circumstances.

I had never gone parachuting, but I felt like I was about to jump out of an airplane. At 5 A.M., I shook my dad's hand and pedaled alone into the cold, wet, black country.

I began slowly, barely able to distinguish the trail ahead, though after a short time my eyes adjusted to the dark and I could see the crushed white limestone in subtle contrast to the dark surroundings. My cycling hat shielded my eyes from the rainfall, and I was able to make out the tree canopy that gradually opened above and ahead. I began to navigate by tracing the canopy line, focusing forward and upward, unlike in normal daytime conditions when I would ride looking forward and down at the ground. This strategy allowed me to pick up speed, until I nearly slammed into a large tree that had fallen and blocked the trail. I had been looking up, but my peripheral vision saved me from a severe accident as I hit the brakes and skidded safely into the side of the tree. Lifting my bike, I climbed over the branches to the other side and continued pedaling, now with more caution. I would have to be slower and more conservative than I had anticipated. I could not risk a ride-ending spill alone in the middle of nowhere.

While I could not see much of anything, my sense of hearing was heightened but did little to help. I heard the gushing and gurgling of water and the shrill hiss of wind and the occasional splinter of a tree falling nearby. The rain crackled in my ears like television fuzz on full blast. The ground was so saturated from the precipitation in the days and weeks before that the new rain was unable to seep into the earth, spilling horizontally once it fell, swelling the creeks and streams, and forming mini waterfalls and mudslides on the embankments along the trail.

My heart jumped when a voice shouted from the darkness. I was so preoccupied with staying on the trail that I had filtered out everything else, including any sense of time. In addition, I could not accurately gauge my pace as I was unable to read the computer on my bike for distance.

"Hey, Ben! Good going!" It was my dad. I had apparently made it to the first trailhead in Calhoun.

I could barely make out his silhouette. It looked as though he were filming my ride under the cover of an umbrella. I swallowed my heart and continued on.

"You okay?" he shouted.

I yelled back, "Yes!"

My hands quickly became numb from the cold rain and wind. Though I could not see it, I occasionally felt the pink wristband on my hand as a reminder and added motivation.

My spirits rose with the first hint of daylight, which was delayed and dulled by heavy cloud cover. I knew I would soon be able to see without actually thinking about it, and eventually warmth, no matter how slight, would come.

Daylight brought its own set of issues, though, as I could now see the horrid trail conditions in lucid detail. Standing water covered the crushed limestone. Leaves, branches, and an occasional fallen tree were strewn about like wreckage. It was now abundantly clear why I seemed to be losing speed. Looking down at my tires, I could see them digging into the soft ground, creating added drag. The trail's compact limestone had been overrun by rain, mud, and earth. Stretches that were already softer in normal conditions were now akin to a sandy beach, providing immense resistance. My skinny road tires, though Kevlar-belted and reliable, were less than ideal as they burrowed deep into the trail. I felt as if I were running a marathon in lead shoes.

In one particularly soft section that cut through a sprawling crop field, the stiff wind met me head-on and slowed my momentum to a crawl. Though I never considered myself a specialist in climbing hills, I always preferred climbing to riding into the wind. The wind was maddening and demoralizing. Not only had I been riding into the wind for some time now, I felt as if I were riding through quicksand. Soon my rear tire began to spin and I could not steer. Forced to dismount from my bike, I looked back at the narrow gulley carved a few inches into the trail by my tires.

I had planned on averaging nearly twenty miles per hour through this first stretch, but now I was forced to walk in conditions that were beyond my control. I had already expended far more energy than I had anticipated, and I was quickly losing ground, physically and mentally.

Cursing the wind and ground, I thought about quitting. I could hear in my head the naysayers who doubted me: *See, we told you this was crazy.* Then I looked at my pink wristband and continued to plod toward the other side of the state like a mule pulling a plow.

When I reached Sedalia, just 35 miles into the ride, I was already a half hour behind my timetable. The trailhead featured a depot, which had been preserved as a railroad heritage museum. My dad, along with a reporter and photographer from the local newspaper, greeted me at the depot under cover from the rain, which continued its pelting onslaught. They looked at me in disbelief, my bike and body encased in layers of silt, mud, and muck.

"How's it going?" the reporter asked with a giddy grin that seemed to suggest I was insane.

I wanted to challenge her to try riding for a few minutes to find out for herself, but somehow I collected myself. "I've expended more energy than I expected, but I'm trying to focus on the positives. The cool temperature is keeping my heart rate in check, and the rain is doing much of my perspiring for me, and that's keeping me hydrated. The clouds are acting like my sunscreen, so I shouldn't have to worry about getting burned today."

My words rolled off my tongue without thought or hesitation. I had not even thought about focusing on the positives until then.

"What's your plan?" she asked. "Are you going to continue riding?"

"I'll be in St. Charles this evening," I said.

She looked at the photographer, and they both shared a grin.

After grabbing more drink, food, and gels from my dad, I sped away from the depot and into town. It was the only point on the entire trail that meandered along paved roads, albeit for less than a mile. Amid the pouring rain, I got lost trying to read the road signs. One driver honked at me as I crossed a road in haste. Eventually, I found the trail again on the north side of town, my pace abruptly slowing when I left the pavement.

Again I was forced to dismount from my bike and trudge through a few more soft sections, but my mood was gradually beginning to lift. The unexpected poise and confidence that had guided my conversation with the reporter now transformed my spirit. As I continued to put the miles behind me, slowly and steadily, I realized that accomplishing my initial objective of setting a new trail record was impossible. Now I needed to be flexible and adapt by modifying my goal to simply completing the trail in one day.

My spirits were doubly raised when I reached Boonville, a modest-sized town seventy-five miles into the ride. Though I was now an hour behind my timetable, for the first time I was content. The rain softened to a drizzle and the sun shone dully through the clouds. I had finally reached the Missouri River. After crossing the Boonville Bridge, I resumed pedaling on the trail, which would now run flat and parallel with the river for the remaining 150 miles east to St. Charles. At one time or another, I had ridden every mile from here to St. Charles. It was all relatively familiar territory, so I felt like I was home free.

Reflecting on the ride thus far, I looked at my pink bracelet and the trail ahead and felt more energized and focused. The rain, clouds, and soft trail became my companions. They pushed me farther and faster, and I suddenly felt at peace and not alone. Some greater energy seemed to be pulling me along, the same indefatigable force that had accompanied Bridget through her fight with cancer, the same spirit that had overcome and inspired me through my encounter with Isaac and my conversations with Father Marco and Father Paul. I felt the power of the Holy Spirit. My newfound drive and motivation were such that under normal trail and weather conditions I knew I would have been a half-hour ahead of my goal. But it did not matter. I was now set to simply ride the trail in one day, a reasonable goal, I rationalized, considering I had been riding on skinny racing tires in a flash flood. I would now focus on conserving energy, as I was unsure of the trail conditions ahead, and be constantly aware of properly refueling my body. I was now riding farther than I ever had in a single day.

The repetitive, rhythmic nature of each pedal stroke reminded me of canoe trips in Canada, when the monotony of every paddle stroke transformed to poetry and prayer. As the weather tempered, my technique and cadence normalized as I had rehearsed on long training rides, pedaling in the saddle for nearly ten minutes between ninety and ninety-five revolutions per minute, then getting out of the saddle and leveraging my pedal stroke with the weight of my body for up to fifty revolutions, then settling back in the saddle for another cycle, constantly resituating my hands on the handlebars to use varying sets of muscles. After topping the century-mile mark, the intense focus and sheer will to finish the trail in one day drove my legs round and round. The pain numbed and I felt supremely alive in the cool misty drizzle and in the company of the gray rumbling clouds still pacing me to the south.

In this contemplative state, the ride became an afterthought. It was as if I were on a spiritual retreat and happened to be riding a bike. I allowed only positive thoughts to enter my mind. *I'd rather be wet from the rain than from profuse sweat in the heat and humidity,* I told myself. *This is keeping my heart rate down and helping me stay hydrated. Hot damn, this is almost like cheating!* Then my mind would drift to our family. *We are incredibly blessed for all we have—God, family, friends, doctors, health insurance, and Herceptin. Thank God for Herceptin!*

In Rocheport, I zoomed through an old railroad tunnel, hollering to hear my echo, then grabbed more fuel from my dad. Two trailheads later, in Jefferson City, the homecoming began. To the south, across the river, the dome of the state capital rose above the town, and at the trailhead, Bridget, our boys, and my parents cheered me on, waving bright pink, yellow, and orange signs.

"Go Daddy, go!" the boys chanted.

As I approached, I could read the signs, which read, "Ride for a Cure," "Go Fast Dad," and one that Andrew created that said, "Dad You're Good."

"You're going to do it!" Bridget said. Her faith in me was invigorating.

The increasing physical difficulty of the ride was somewhat offset by the mental lift from my family. Then, about forty miles later, in Rhineland, just outside of Hermann, Sandy and Dave showed up to join the crew, and thereafter more friends and family appeared at each new trailhead.

Several months earlier, I had ridden this final stretch of sixty-plus miles in just over three hours. I realized it would now take much longer.

Though I had done a fairly good job of blocking it out, my physical condition was deteriorating. The slow trail had consumed precious energy that I had planned on having in reserve for the last few hours. My body was in dire need of rest, screaming for me to stop.

With thirty-five miles left, I approached the Dutzow trailhead and saw in the distance a cyclist standing next to his bike on the trail. Clad in a white biking jersey, black shorts, and a white hat, the cyclist was flanked by a growing group of supporters.

"DuMont!" the cyclist shouted from afar. It was the unmistakable voice of Tutts. His timing could not have been better.

When I reached him, we briefly exchanged greetings and set off. I shadowed his rear wheel, capitalizing on every possible square inch of his draft. It was all I could do to hang on and ride the train.

The rain continued to fall, albeit more lightly than the morning downpour, and the fading of daylight began to accelerate with the heavy cloud cover.

"Dude, this trail sucks!" Tutts said. "I feel like we should be going twenty miles an hour, but we're only doing fifteen."

Not only had there been nobody on the trail that day, there were also no dogs, which was very uncharacteristic. Typically on a long ride I would encounter a few farm dogs, or even some strays, and they would inevitably chase me. The weather had kept all of the canines tucked away under cover.

With about twenty-five miles left, we stopped for a break.

"Babe, are you okay?" Bridget asked as I stepped off my bike.

I was feeling a little lightheaded and my speech was becoming somewhat slurred, but I wanted to have some fun with it, so I pretended to stumble and nearly collapse.

"Honey!" she said suddenly, lunging to grab me.

I looked at her and grinned, then chuckled. "Just kidding!"

My joke did not go over well, as Bridget was very nervous about my condition. I remembered my failed attempt to make light of my racing accident when I had broken my collarbone. It would be the first and last prank I pulled that day.

More friends and family were cheering us on at the few remaining trailheads, beginning in Augusta. As we neared each trailhead and heard the cheers, a rush of adrenaline coursed through my veins and increased my cadence.

I became distracted, however, and lazy about properly refueling my body. I was not consuming as much, and in turn my muscles were rebelling and locking up. My world was my body, and my body was in agony. Every muscle was scorched. My arms and shoulders had acted like shock absorbers the entire day. Riding on the rough surface had jolted my hands, wrists, forearms, arms, shoulders, and back like a jackhammer.

The sky darkened when we were about ten miles outside of St. Charles, and it was quiet as we rode along the river through thick air teeming with large pockets of gnats and mosquitoes.

"I can't even see the trail!" Tutts shouted back several times.

Somehow, he was able to navigate through the blackness. Any ambient light from the town or hint of starlight was blocked by the thick canopy of tree cover surrounding the trail. I stayed on Tutts' rear wheel, my eyes locked on his white jersey.

After we rode under the towering interstate bridge, the lights of St. Charles began to poke through the thinning tree canopy. We passed the casino and auditorium and, finally, after riding through a last wooded stretch, the trail opened up on all sides. A small crowd was gathered a few hundred yards away at the last trailhead. In between the crowd and us was a kid on a bike. As we approached, it became evident that it was Jack.

When he saw us, he yelled "They're here!" back at everybody, then he hopped on his bike and rode in front of us at a frenetic pace. Jack scared me he was riding so fast. I was concerned about him taking a spill and had to tell him to slow down. Nonetheless, he led us flawlessly to the finish.

After 225 miles and sixteen hours, I had made it. I set my bike down and lifted Jack up and kissed him. Bridget made her way over to me and we embraced. A light from a television camera was pointed in my eye, making it hard to see who was in the crowd, but I could hear their voices. My parents, brother, grandma, aunts, uncles, friends, and nearly all of Bridget's family were there. They had been tracking my progress during the day through updates from my dad and Bridget.

I stood amid the flock of supporters, not sure what to say. While I was grateful for the support, I was uncomfortable with the attention. I had never relished the limelight, and I felt somewhat awkward.

After thanking everybody, I shouted weakly, "I survived, but Bridget is the real survivor."

I was not sure many even heard me over the noise of the crowd.

As everybody began to leave, Tutts looked at me and laughed in disbelief. "What were you thinking? Those were thirty-five of the hardest miles I've ever ridden, and you were riding all day."

My bike was completely encrusted in mud, soot, and limestone. It felt good to take my shoes and socks off and feel the cool rock surface on my bare feet, and even better when I sat in the car, the first time I had sat since 5 A.M.

On the ride home, Bridget insisted we stop by McDonald's for a couple cheeseburgers. I consumed them both in just a couple of minutes.

When we arrived home, I stepped onto the driveway, which was cool, even cold, on my feet, and a sudden case of the chills overcame me. I thought it was the change in temperature from the warm car and heater blowing on my feet to the cool pavement, or maybe the process of my body and heart rate coming down from the day. Either way, I began to shiver, and my teeth chattered uncontrollably.

My mom, concerned, followed me as I struggled up the steps inside, then my dad stood guard outside the bathroom as I took a shower.

I went to bed with a winter cap to stave off the chills. My dad and I talked for several minutes, and I could tell his concern had turned to relief that the day was over with a safe and successful ending.

Before he left me alone, he said, "Don't ever let anybody tell you that you can't do something. You will prove them wrong."

I suddenly felt like a youngster again, as if I had received straight A's on my report card and made my dad proud. I got a little choked up. Then I consumed an entire supreme pizza, two oranges, one banana, and two bottles of Gatorade, and slept for twelve hours.

# KOMENTUCKY DERBY

\* \* \*

A couple of weeks after my ride, we participated in
Bridget's second Komen Race for the Cure. The previous year Bridget was so sick from the chemotherapy that
she was unable to walk more than a few hundred feet before
we had to leave. Dozens of friends and family joined us in
the walk. Bridget had named her team "Bridget's Brigade"
from the suggestion of our brother-in-law Don, who served
a brief stint in the military. One of her grade-school friends,
Andee, designed custom camouflage T-shirts with pink lettering for her team. More than sixty thousand walked in the
event. When we reached the top of an incline in downtown
St. Louis, we could see the masses stretched out before us like
an undulating pink ribbon of humanity covering every speck
of street. It was incredibly moving.

We hosted a party that evening at a nearby lakeside club-
house. More than one hundred friends and family who had
supported us over the past sixteen months attended. It was our
way of thanking them and celebrating the success of Bridget's
treatment, which was nearly complete. The chemotherapy, surgery, and radiation had all done their part. Now she had only a
few more drug treatments left. Herceptin, which did not have
the ill effects of the chemotherapy, had been the keystone to

her successful outcome. Now Bridget's hair was growing back again and her strength and energy were slowly rebounding. El Hombre had hit the "grand slam" he had hoped for through an aggressive treatment plan.

I had prepared some remarks for the event. Public speaking had never been my forte. I dreaded it, but I found the words flowed off my tongue with ease when I talked about Bridget. I focused my talk on three key characteristics that defined her throughout her bout with cancer: strength, faith, and openness. She had remained strong in her fight, faithful to Our Lord, and open in sharing her story to raise awareness and offer hope to others struggling with cancer. Through her own experience, she taught Jack and Andrew how to handle obstacles with dignity, grace, and resilience, and they would be better off for it when they grew up.

The party was celebratory in every sense and, for Bridget and me, an unofficial "goodbye" to cancer. It was a day we had dreamed of for more than a year, our opportunity to share with our loved ones a good-riddance to Bridget's illness. The disease had consumed much of our lives, dictating what we did, controlling our emotions, and turning our agendas on end. Now it was time to regain some normalcy in our lives. Bridget had been unable to work for a long time, but now she was tutoring again and resuming her sewing business and selling stationery as a sales rep for a paper company. We felt an indescribable sense of relief and gratitude. Bridget had beaten the odds. She had defeated cancer, thanks to a quality team of medical professionals, the miracle of medicine, the grace of God, and her own grit and determination. It was a total team effort. Our friends and family had kept us afloat with their support and prayers, and our parents continued to help with the mounting medical bills, which provided us peace of mind. While I had imagined Bridget's illness as a shipwreck on occasion, now

I felt us heading toward shore—and safety—aboard a rescue boat filled with all of our supporters.

After the party, the stress and chaos of our lives gradually came to a halt, and we were left with something we had missed for a long while—free time. We finally had time to do things without cancer at the forefront. We relished our lives now, as they once had been, though we were changed, different. We cherished the blessing of our boys more and spent more time with them, reading to them, playing with them in the backyard, and taking them to the park. No longer taking our health for granted, we transitioned to healthier eating habits, replacing much of the processed junk with organic food and more fruits and vegetables. Our faith had strengthened. We were emboldened by God, and Bridget felt the need to do more for others. She volunteered her time with the American Cancer Society, consulting with recently diagnosed patients, offering them hope through her own experience, spending hours on the phone with other women who felt they had no chance. Still, she wanted to do more. She did not want others to experience what she had, and so she set out to raise more money to fight cancer.

In the fall, Bridget and I went to the horse races in Illinois with some friends. It was the first time we had been to the track, and we had as much fun watching the crowd as the races. Near the end of the night, the girls were talking about hosting a derby party the following year. The guys all smirked when they talked about colorful derby hats and pretty decorations and sophisticated drinks.

"I could host a derby party and use it to raise funds for charity," Bridget said.

She wanted to support Susan G. Komen. The girls all latched on to the idea. One of them was a graphic designer and agreed to create a logo and invitation for the event. Others offered to solicit donations and items for a silent auction.

After our night at the races, Bridget continued to talk about hosting a derby party as a fundraiser. Through my work on our school's auction, I knew how time-consuming event planning could be. Though I was open to the idea, I warned her about the amount of time and effort it would take to be successful.

"That's okay," she said.

Once I knew she was serious and determined to pull it off, I helped her with brainstorming and planning. Just a couple of weeks after our night at the races, she visited a winery to see if they would host a derby party for us. When Bridget returned home, she was smiling.

"They agreed to host the party for us, free of charge," she said. "They'll also arrange for discounted food and drinks and have live entertainment."

The winery was the newest venue of its kind, to the west of St. Louis, beautifully situated amid the rolling green and open valleys adjacent to the Missouri River, near the Katy Trail. It boasted a spacious interior and a huge, multi-level outdoor deck with a broad vantage of the vineyard that spread out below on a gentle hill. At the bottom of the hill rested a small pond, which reflected the vast lushness of the countryside beyond.

Bridget's grand idea was slowly gaining traction. Now she needed a name for it. I spent several days thumbing through the thesaurus and pondering name possibilities, until I thought about simply combining Komen with Kentucky Derby. The result was The Komentucky Derby. Thankfully, Bridget liked the name, my only significant contribution to the event. She and her friends took over the planning from that point. It was best to let them do their thing. They were event planners, self-starters, and I knew they would be successful. I took on more responsibilities around the house so Bridget could dedicate more time to her planning.

We hosted the inaugural Komentucky Derby the following spring, and it exceeded expectations, with a hundred attendees and about fifteen thousand dollars raised. Rain had been in the forecast for the day, and drizzle greeted guests as they arrived. The clouds, however, parted in the early afternoon, and as if by divine intervention, the sun shone brilliantly on the winery throughout the day. It served as a metaphor not only for the day and its bright, upbeat mood, but for Bridget's survival experience. She would not let anything get in her way or dampen her spirit.

Friends and family had fun with the theme and dressed in derby attire with colorful hats, dresses, bow ties, and slick blazers. They enjoyed wine and appetizers and desserts. A band played mellow, upbeat tunes outside on the deck as everybody perused the auction items and socialized. Several of our friends served as volunteers collecting money for derby betting and raffles. A local television crew appeared to interview Bridget for the evening news. She smiled and seemed to glow when she spoke. The winery staff was accommodating and pleased with the turnout and publicity.

After the event, a large group met at a nearby restaurant and bar. Relaxing, we sat with dozens of others and watched my friend Jim sing karaoke to U2's "With or Without You" in a voice remarkably like Bono's, and soon the restaurant owner was among us, curious about all of the flowery hats. He was so moved by Bridget and her story that he gave our party a discount, made a donation to the Komentucky Derby, and agreed to host the after-party for the following year. The sun seemed to follow Bridget throughout the day. Good things had been born from her good will.

# PART FOUR

# RENEWAL

**\* \* \***

In the week immediately following Bridget's diagnosis, my faith had been tested. The worry, stress, and fear that had riddled my being for seven long days were amplified with feelings of desertion, even betrayal by God. At the time, I did not know how my faith could recover—or if it would—but He, the One by whom I had felt abandoned, showed me strength and resilience in ways I had never before experienced or imagined.

On a warm spring day, I stood in the basement of our church before dozens of retreatants, all of their eyes fixed on me. I was nervous but eager to tell my story.

"About six months ago," I began, "I was sitting where you are now. I remember on the first day of our retreat, our lay director tapped me on the shoulder and said that my wife had called and said that somebody had broken into our house. After I phoned Bridget and learned that everything was okay, I didn't think about it again until I returned home the next day. I was so enveloped in the moment on our retreat because I truly felt in the presence of Jesus Christ. It was such an awesome feeling, and the best part was I knew it was real and authentic. For me, the retreat was a genuine and powerful renewal experience. I hope you have a similar experience. If you have an open mind and heart, I know you will."

The topic of my talk, or testimonial, was renewal.

"So, what is renewal?" I continued. "To me, renewal means rebirth, conversion, or reawakening in a sometimes unexpected moment or moments of clarity. In the fullest sense, it is not an end in and of itself, but rather the catalyst for continued growth and spiritual fulfillment.

"While I feel like Christ has been a part of my entire life, He has become more real and apparent in the past couple of years, particularly due to one significant, life-changing experience of renewal."

I told the group about Bridget's bout with cancer, my visions, and my faith journey, beginning with my interactions with Isaac. As I spoke, my voice that at first cracked with nervousness became impassioned. What had been my greatest fear, public speaking, became something with which I was almost comfortable, or at least did not mind. I felt compelled to tell how I had become enlightened through my own experience of renewal, how the Holy Spirit had transformed our lives, and I was not going to let my own phobia of public speaking get in the way.

"As I progress into the next chapter of my life," I concluded, "I continue to be thankful for the little things and the not-so-little things, like my faith, my beautiful wife—a healthy survivor now for more than two years—and our two boys. I am truly humbled and wonder how I can be so lucky. In all of my thanks and praise, I am still struck by Isaac, an unpretentious, ordinary man who did something truly extraordinary through the power of the Holy Spirit. When I reflect about that day shortly after Bridget's diagnosis when Isaac confronted me, my emotions get the better of me, because I become overwhelmed with peace, love, confidence, and fearlessness…and my soul sings."

Bridget had put me up to it.

She had participated in the women's retreat at our parish one year after her diagnosis. She was so moved by the experience that she helped to give the next retreat with her fellow retreatants. In preparation, she met every week for several hours with her retreat sisters, and together they discussed Scripture and grew in their faith as they planned the event. The retreat was a two-day event at the parish. It focused on cultivating a relationship with Jesus Christ and was highlighted by a series of reflections from those who were putting on the retreat.

Each reflection had a theme, and Bridget's focused on "community." She spent hours preparing for her weekly meetings and then composing her presentation. Amid all of her responsibilities, including recovering from cancer, taking care of the kids, resuming her sewing business, and tutoring students, she made time to dedicate to God. It had become more important to her than ever. She was now channeling the same energy and vigor that she had used to defeat cancer to grow in her faith. After her retreat, she began going to Bible study and even encouraged some of her friends to attend with her. She eventually started her own Bible study group with several friends and hosted weekly meetings at our house.

Following her retreat at our parish, Bridget encouraged me to participate in the men's retreat, and though I put it off for several months, she eventually insisted that I go. She was well intentioned, and I knew I had to get out of my comfort zone. I had felt rich with my own spirituality inside for a long time, but now I needed to break out of my shell. It was difficult to open up to a bunch of grown men whom I did not know, but after the retreat, I realized it had all been worth it. These men became my brothers, guys who had been through difficult times like myself, brothers who shared a common love for

Christ, men who, after our retreat, demanded hugs instead of handshakes when I saw them at Church.

In addition to the parish retreat, I joined an alumni group at our school that focused on Ignatian Spirituality. Based on the teachings of St. Ignatius, this spirituality for everyday life maintained that God is omnipresent in our world and engaged in our lives. Ignatian Spirituality served as a pathway to deeper prayer, good decisions guided by keen discernment, and an active life of service to others. One of the Jesuits at our school was the spiritual moderator for our group and guided our monthly discussions, which began with Mass at the school at 6:45 A.M. Though it was tough to wake up, I always looked forward to it, and it became one of the highlights of each month.

Our group was an outgrowth of the annual alumni retreat, which I attended shortly after the parish retreat. The retreat center was situated along the Mississippi River and offered serene, peaceful grounds and scenic views of the mighty river, wildlife, and misty sunrises. It was a powerful and moving experience, peaceful and introspective. The spiritual director, a Jesuit, encouraged us to read a section of the Bible and envision ourselves at the scene, just as St. Ignatius used to do. I read the entire Gospel of John and immersed myself in the story as a bystander, deeply moved by the undying love of Jesus Christ. With every word, everything seemed to make perfect sense, both in Jesus' time and in the present, because He radiated with such peace, hope, compassion, and incredible clarity. His spirit was limitless and timeless, and I could feel its enduring intensity.

During one afternoon on a break, I ventured outside. It had just snowed a few days earlier, and the temperature hovered in the low teens. I followed the railroad tracks that separated the retreat house from the river, and began to run south, jogging on the crunchy snow between the railroad ties, my breath visible in the dry, frigid air. After a few miles, I began to sweat and rested on a rock-strewn beach along the river. I took off my wool hat, coat, and shirt, my wet hair instantly icing over. It was a clear day, and the sun felt good on my skin, my body steaming. The hulking hunks of ice crashed into one another in the river with deep raucous thuds, and occasionally tree branches on the shore snapped under the weight of ice and sounded like the shatter of glass.

I pulled a piece of paper from my coat pocket. It was a retreat handout. I had been carrying it with me the past couple of days and would regularly look at it, the words simple yet immeasurable in their impact and meaning. St. Ignatius had written his renowned *Spiritual Exercises*—a series of prayers, meditations, and mental exercises—five centuries ago, and on the paper was his document's first principle and foundation. It was the cornerstone to his philosophy and spirituality:

The goal of our life is to live with God forever.
God, who loves us, gave us life.
Our own response of love allows God's life
to flow into us without limit.

All the things in this world are gifts from God,
Presented to us so that we can know God more easily
and make a return of love more readily.
As a result, we appreciate and use all these gifts of God
Insofar as they help us to develop as loving persons.
But if any of these gifts become the center of our lives,
They displace God
And so hinder our growth toward our goal.

In everyday life, then, we must hold ourselves in balance
Before all of these created gifts insofar as we have a
choice
And are not bound by some obligation.
We should not fix our desires on health or sickness,
Wealth or poverty, success or failure, a long life or a
short one.
For everything has the potential of calling forth in us
A deeper response to our life in God.

Our only desire and our one choice should be this:
I want and I choose what better leads
To God's deepening his life in me.

As I pondered in the peacefulness, reveling in the beauty
of nature and the words of St. Ignatius, my thoughts floated
upward, thankful for Jesus Christ and everybody who had been
a positive force in my life, particularly Bridget and all who ral-
lied behind us through her illness. I realized they were all conduits for the infinite love of God, and I became overwhelmed
by gratitude. When I thought about Isaac and the impact he
had had on my life by reaching out during a time of need, I
felt renewed, invigorated, and fulfilled. My faith and spirituality, which had wavered after Bridget's diagnosis, had not only
healed but they flourished and thrived, like a scar that grows
over stronger than the original, unblemished skin.

On the run back to the retreat house, I seemed to float
over the crunchy snow and railroad ties, up the icy hill and
beyond the religious statues that were decorated by snow.

A first-time retreatant traditionally talked about his experience to the group, and so I was asked to give a presentation
to everybody. The thought of public speaking still made me
cringe with anxiety. I decided to keep my message simple with

three examples of how I had felt the power and love of Christ the past few days—through the fellowship of the other men, through my reading of the Bible, and through my experience in the beautiful yet freezing outdoors.

After I spoke, one man told me, "Great job. You should be a public speaker."

I had clearly been moved by something far greater than myself.

# THE CHALLENGE

*** 

In the fall, Bridget and I went to her friend Annie's house for a party. Her husband Joe and I shared a passion for cycling. He was a "gear guy" and had several different bikes for road racing, off road, and recreation. We had once taken our bikes on a train to Hermann, the quaint old German town along the Missouri River, then ridden the Katy Trail for the sixty-five miles back to St. Louis. It was an ideal ride, a perfect blend of challenge and recreation, enough to get the blood moving, but not enough to prohibit taking in and appreciating the beauty of the trail and scenery.

"Hey, buddy," Joe said when I saw him. "You been riding much?"

I had been spending a lot of time canoeing with my cousin Jon, my cycling mentor. A bad knee had ended his amateur racing career, and our shared love for canoeing inspired us to take up racing on the water. Jon bought a sleek race canoe, which we named "Magis." After regularly training on a nearby lake and river, we entered a couple of races on the Missouri River. Jon and I fared well and were planning to race in the MR340, a 340-mile race on the Missouri from Kansas City to St. Louis, but it had been cancelled due to flooding.

I explained this to Joe but told him I hoped to do some riding again soon.

"You gonna do the ride again?" he asked with a grin.

"Which ride? The one from Hermann?"

"The big one. The ride across the state."

I chuckled. "Yeah, right."

"Seriously."

"I wasn't planning on it, but I always said if I ever did it again, I'd have to ride the entire thing with somebody else and have better trail conditions."

"I'll ride with you."

Joe was not laughing anymore.

"Right on," I said, and we shook hands.

# WINDY DEFEAT

\* \* \*

I began to get back in riding shape early in the year. I had been doing P90X, an intense home exercise program, and continued with the leg and core exercises to complement my riding regimen. I was training with more confidence and experience than ever. Joe recruited two other cyclists, his brother Mike and Tutts, to help him pace me throughout the day. I planned to ride in early May, as opposed to the summer, to take advantage of cooler weather. The trail had been extended to 237 miles since my first ride. I was hoping to become the first to make the entire trek in one day on the "new" trail, something I emphasized to help with my fundraising effort for Bridget's Brigade.

As the day of the ride neared, the availability of my support team diminished. I would be riding the first seventy-five miles solo, though I did not mind, as I would have fresh legs and likely not need drafting assistance early in the day. My parents again made the trip from Virginia to support me. Bridget drove me to Clinton on the west side of the state the day before the ride and served as my support crew, and my parents took Jack and Andrew to meet up with us later in the day.

The first seventy-five miles went well, much better than the first time. I had the luxury of wearing a headlamp, compliments of Joe, to see the trail in the dark. When the sun rose, a giant blanket of fog encased the meadows and farmland, punctuating the beauty of the rolling land. Near Boonville my mind turned to meditation. I contemplated the Holy Trinity as three deer appeared next to the trail, bounding alongside me gracefully, flawlessly, all springing and bouncing in tandem with one another, united as one cohesive unit. It was mesmerizing to watch them work together—peacefully, seamlessly, enchantingly like the divine mystery. They had no fear of me as I pedaled but seemed instead to be cheering me on, pushing me further and faster.

King Tutts met me in Boonville, and from there we rode about ten miles on a paved road parallel to a portion of the trail closed for maintenance. We sped on the smooth surface that cut through open expanses of corn and wheat fields until the wind began to push us from the side, slowing us considerably. I was trying to stay close to King Tutts' back tire to catch his draft without veering into the road. It became physically and mentally draining, and while the road surface was a pleasant change, it included a long, steep hill just before returning to the trail. The black asphalt was a magnet for the sweltering sun, and we baked in the heat emanating from it.

I was hoping the trail would provide protection from the gathering wind, but it seemed to act like a tunnel, funneling the air like a jet engine and confronting us head on. Tutts' draft had little benefit, as the wind began to swirl from all directions but behind. While the wind typically came from the west, it was now blowing directly from the east, the direction we were heading. When Tutts got a flat tire, he insisted I move on. He would hitch a ride from the next trailhead and meet me somewhere ahead. The wind was bending large trees, and small branches and leaves were whirling around like tornado debris. The rolling resistance of the trail, coupled with the fierce wind, was making progress intolerably slow. It became a struggle to maintain a speed of twelve miles per hour.

In Jefferson City, I met up with Joe and his brother, but by then I had sapped my energy reserves, and their draft was providing no protection from the impenetrable wind. Moreover, they were continually outpacing me. As we neared Hermann, it was getting late in the day, and the wind only intensified. The sun and wind had taken their toll on my body, and I was feeling lightheaded, nauseated, and dehydrated.

In Rhineland, just outside the old German town, I put my bike down in defeat after 175 miles.

"This wind is unbelievable," my dad said. "You have no reason to hang your head."

Jack was crying. He had brought his bike and wanted to cross the finish with me as he had done two years ago. I consoled him as I struggled to deal with the situation myself. Something did not feel right with my body, but most of all, I was frustrated with the conditions. I had never experienced such forceful wind from the east. On the drive home, I looked at flags and trees and grass whipping in the wind, which handily pushed our minivan from side to side.

"Don't feel bad," Bridget said. "They say the wind gusts are forty miles an hour. Nobody could do the ride today, not against that wind for that distance."

She felt the defeat like I did, for she had sacrificed a lot to make me successful. Riding for me, particularly after Bridget's diagnosis, had been therapeutic, and she did everything she could to support me. Even through the agony of her chemotherapy, she had encouraged me to continue cycling, and once she digested the concept of my riding across the state in one day, she abandoned her worry and anxiety to become my champion and cheerleader.

"He'll be fine," Bridget said, referring to Jack. "He just wanted to cross the finish line with his daddy today."

# TORNADO

\* \* \*

I was pedaling before dawn on the limestone trail, settling into a steady, comfortable cadence, my headlamp illuminating the way. After the sun rose, the mist that blanketed the rolling countryside disappeared slowly, imperceptibly. I passed six trailheads before arriving in Boonville in the late morning, then biked over the bridge and rode east along the trail that hugged the Missouri River. After chugging through the old railway tunnel in Rocheport and past another few trailheads, I arrived in Jefferson City at about noon. I had ridden more than a hundred miles solo.

Just a few days after my failed attempt, I made plans for another shot later in the month, much to the dismay of Bridget, my parents, and others. I had committed too much to the ride and felt too good to be content with having my effort stymied by gusty misfortune. Bridget knew what the ride had meant to me and again made the sacrifice to be my support crew. This time Dave, Bridget's stepdad, joined us as well to help as part of the support team for another try at the 237-mile trail in one day.

Joe joined me in Jefferson City, and from there I rode behind him to take advantage of his draft. I was on track to finish early in the evening as I had planned, but my condition was beginning to decline. While the stiff wind did not match its previous intensity, the elements were again taking their toll on me. The sun and humidity sapped my energy, and I felt sluggish sooner than expected. I became somewhat nauseated and lightheaded. My stomach was upset, and my body felt overheated. Something seemed strangely out of whack as I struggled to keep up with Joe. I had ridden this far several times before yet never felt so bad.

As we passed through the trailheads in Tebbetts, Mokane, Portland, Bluffton, and Rhineland, the sky began to darken behind us from the southwest. We had been warned of the possibility of light showers later in the day, but the forecast changed as the day progressed. Bridget confirmed that strong storms were fast approaching.

"Hey, man, any thunder or lightning and I'm out of here," Joe told me definitively.

"I respect that," I said. "But the only thing that's pulling me from the trail is a tornado."

When we reached the Hermann area, nearly 180 miles from Clinton, around the same spot I had stopped only three weeks earlier, the clouds closed the curtain on the sun. It began sprinkling, and soon the thunder and lightning commenced. Supercells were forming, and the wind was picking up with ferocity.

"Dude, I'm bailing!" Joe yelled.

I looked back and shouted, "You okay?"

"I'll be fine," he said, motioning for Dave to pick him up in his car.

I pedaled onward. About five miles later the drizzle turned to rain, and hail followed immediately after. I was wearing a helmet, and thought that would protect my head from the falling iceballs.

Just minutes after the hailstorm began, Bridget pulled the minivan in front of me on a road that intersected the trail to block my way.

"Get in the car," she said emphatically with the window rolled down.

After some protests, I threw my bike in the back of the minivan and climbed in the front passenger's seat, which was totally saturated from just a couple seconds with the door open. The hail sounded as if it was going to annihilate the vehicle, rattling like a machine gun just inches from our heads. The sound was deafening.

"It's not worth it, babe," said Bridget, focused on getting out of the storm. "I don't want you to die raising money because you're thankful that I lived."

Joe was a few minutes ahead of us in his car with Dave. We were trying to catch up to them, unable to see more than fifty feet ahead through the onslaught of hail.

On the ride home, I began to feel sick. My head spun and I felt like vomiting. I also felt a constant need to urinate. I had felt the same just a few weeks earlier before I had to bail from the ride. I did not know what was causing this. My stomach was painfully bloated.

"Just tell me to pull over and I will," Bridget said numerous times on the winding two-lane road.

"Just get me home. Let's just get home and I'll be fine."

I had to make three pit stops. At a McDonald's, I looked like somebody who had found civilization after being lost for weeks, with a sunburnt face that revealed dread and defeat, wicked cycling sunglasses, cycling shorts, jersey half-zipped up, and cycling shoes that clinked as I walked. When a man exited the bathroom and saw me, he said, "Holy crap, dude. You okay?"

My pit stops delayed our ride home and allowed the brewing storm to catch up and overtake us. Visibility decreased to just a few feet, and highway traffic came to a halt. Somehow, we were able to exit and duck beneath cover at a gas station, along with twenty other vehicles crammed into the space.

Jack and Andrew were back in St. Louis at their baseball games. We had planned for them to join the celebration at the end of the Katy Trail when I finished. Now Bridget was talking to her family and friends on her phone to rearrange plans and ensure the boys were taken care of, meanwhile trying to gauge the storm and tend to me. She was bouncing back and forth, trying to focus on each equally—phone conversation, the storm, and me. Even as my condition was deteriorating, the storm was demanding everybody's utmost attention. Panic and worry marked the eyes of everybody hunkered in their cars. One woman made a mad dash for the convenience store door, yelling into the wind as she tromped through the water. A human-sized chunk of billboard whizzed across the parking lot and slammed into the store with a piercing thud. Bridget was learning about the storm from others in St. Louis.

"It's a tornado," Bridget said.

It had come without warning and was instantly the focus of every media outlet.

"We'll get out of this storm, and we'll be okay," I said, fearing our car would get slammed by another chunk of billboard or the aluminum cover above us that was fluttering in the violent wind.

I spoke calmly, masking my pain and intensifying desperation. My innards were screaming in agony, writhing in pain, and my mind was terrified of the storm that was gathering in strength and speed and power. Looking at the fear of the others in their cars around us, I felt like a cow in a corral with dozens of others, dreadfully awaiting the slaughterhouse. I had never felt fear as I had at that moment, yet the pain I was experiencing in my body surpassed that fear.

After an hour at the gas station, the wind and hail relented, transitioning to rain, and we hopped back on the highway. Shortly thereafter, the sky opened up, and a definitive line marked the contrast between a deep cloudless blue to the south and east and thick black swirling clouds to the north and behind us to the west.

"I've gotta get home," I managed to say. "Just gotta get home. Once I get home, I know I'll be fine."

"I'm doing my best, babe," Bridget said.

When we neared our exit from the highway, just fifteen minutes from our house, I told Bridget to focus more on the road.

"Honey, get behind that car right there," I said, pointing to a car ahead to the right. "You need to get in that car's draft. Get in that car's draft. That car right there."

"I'm doing just fine, babe. You're not making any sense."

I was relieved to finally get off the highway, though my need to urinate had become unbearable and overtook the feeling that I was going to get sick. Bridget pulled over at yet another gas station, but there was a long bathroom line, and I immediately raced back to the car.

"Let's just go, just get me home," I said with more urgency than before.

Bridget asked me several questions, and I simply did not respond. In a zoned-out state, I felt as if I was levitating, and time seemed to skip. When we finally reached our house I felt totally relieved, though still very sick and bloated.

Bridget was going to drop me off and pick up the boys from their ball games. When she saw me stumbling inside, she kept the engine running and followed me in to ensure I was okay.

My body began to feel numb and weightless, and when I leaned over to unbuckle my cycling shoes I nearly fell over.

"Here, sit down," Bridget said, pulling over a stool in the kitchen.

As she unfastened my shoes and took them off, I felt myself losing control of my senses and ability to move. When I stood to head upstairs and take a shower, my arms flailed wildly and my legs gave out.

"Ben!" Bridget screamed.

# LAST RITES

* * *

I was in a hospital room talking to a Jesuit priest who was with David, our school's president. They were standing at the foot of the bed where I lay. Father Ralph said a prayer over me, and I shook his hand before the two left.

Some time later, I saw Sandy and Dave in the hospital room. I wasn't sure where I was. I thought I had been dreaming, but they were still standing there, just beside the bed.

"Where am I?"

"You're at the hospital," Sandy said. "You're going to be okay."

"What? What happened?"

"Just get some rest," she replied. "We'll get Bridget."

As they left the room, I realized I was strapped to the metal bed rails and IVs were stuck in my arms.

Soon Bridget came to my side. She said I had had a grand mal seizure when we came home after my bike ride the day before. I had fallen to the ground when she was trying to help take off my shoes. I began to moan loudly, foam spewing from my mouth as I thrashed around violently. Two neighbors rushed over to assist and hold me down. Bridget called the ambulance. When the paramedics arrived, she told them that I had ridden my bike nearly two hundred miles earlier in the day. They thought I needed fluids and immediately hooked me up to an IV. My condition quickly declined when I arrived at the hospital. My brain swelled, and the ER doctors were concerned about the long-term effects. They realized the fluids were not helping and took a blood test, which confirmed my dangerously low sodium level. The doctors then agreed it would be best to put me in an induced coma for twenty-four hours so that my body could recover from the shock and trauma. I was not responding to the tranquilizers, and it took three different types of medication to put me under.

During the initial few hours in the ICU, before the medication put me in a coma, I was in a hazy state of unconsciousness and unabated belligerence. The medical staff was unable to contain or control me. It took six people to wrestle me to the hospital bed, and they applied straps to my hands and feet on the metal bed railing. They also taped gigantic mitts on my hands so that I could not undo the straps. Finally, when I was in the coma—a long oxygen tube fed down my throat directly into my lungs, and medication and fluids, including sodium, fed to me intravenously into a central line in my neck—everybody waited nervously in anticipation. The doctors took a wait-and-see approach. They had no idea how I would recover from the trauma, or if I could.

Bridget said three priests had given me a special blessing. It seemed to her they were reading me my last rites.

"That's right," I told her in a rare moment of lucidity. "I remember talking to Father Ralph when he was here."

"That's impossible because you were unconscious when he was here. You were in a coma."

"Was he here with David?" I asked.

"Yes," she said, surprised, "but how did you know?"

"I was talking to them, and I shook Father Ralph's hand."

"That never happened," she said, shaking her head.

I wondered how I had known about and vividly experienced their presence in my comatose state, especially when nobody had told me about it.

Over the next few days I recovered in the ICU. I was surprised that given the amount of riding I had done, my legs were not sore but my back and shoulder screamed in agony. I had done some serious muscle damage and thrown my arm out of its socket in trying to free myself from the bed and fighting with the doctors and nurses. Morphine did little to numb the pain. Bridget said I had used some choice language as well throughout the ordeal, cursing the medical personnel and even her mom. I had no recollection of any of it.

My short-term memory was shot. I asked Bridget several times what had happened, then drifted off to sleep, only to awake and ask her the same question again. Apparently I had really scared a lot of people. Things had been touch-and-go for a while. Bridget said when the tranquilizers were not working and I was not fighting with the medics, I was riding an imaginary bike in the hospital bed. When I awoke from the coma, I felt imprisoned and claustrophobic, yanking the tube from my mouth and trying to escape, then telling Bridget to get some scissors and cut me out of there. "Just get some scissors, seriously," I pleaded again and again.

The doctor prescribed some light walking to aid my recovery, so Bridget and I did several laps around the floor. Aside from my injured shoulder and back and fuzzy memory, I felt fine, as if I could jog. On the fourth day, the doctor said I was okay to leave. When I saw him, he looked strangely familiar, like an old, long-lost friend, even though I had only met him after I awoke from the coma in a foggy state of mind.

"How are you doing?" I asked as if we were reuniting for the first time after twenty years.

"Fine," he said, smiling. As he began talking, I interrupted him.

"I know you," I said. "Where do I know you from?"

He looked at Bridget and they laughed.

"A few days ago you were trying to beat him up," Bridget said. "Don't worry, you didn't know what you were doing."

"It's good to see you are doing better," said the doc, who gave me strict instructions not to drive for two weeks, not to go to work for one week, not to lift anything heavier than ten pounds, and to generally take it easy for some time.

I soon learned that the storm that had cut my ride short was a spin-off system of what became known as the Joplin Tornado. It was in that small southwestern Missouri town that the tornado had done most of its damage. The tornado razed a wide path through Joplin, destroying everything in its way and killing 158 people. It was the nation's deadliest single tornado in about sixty years.

I did not have it so bad after all, even in my beleaguered state. No longer was I stewing over my consistently bad luck with the weather. I was grateful to Bridget. Her decision to walk me into the house had saved my life. Unaware of the danger of overhydration, I had been drinking too many fluids and no electrolytes after my ride. Our minivan was stuffed with bikes and coolers and gear and supplies, and the only food or drink accessible were several bottles of water. What should have been an hour drive home had turned into a three-hour ordeal because of the tornado. During that time, I was literally watering down my system, unaware of my lethally low sodium levels. I had begun to hallucinate before we reached our house. Thankfully, Bridget arrested my fall before I smacked the ground in our kitchen, and she then called for help. Fluids administered by the paramedics had worsened my condition, though nobody was aware at the time that more fluids could have killed me.

When I learned about my lack of sodium, I recalled that I had been using a new sports drink throughout my ride. I assumed it had ample electrolytes, but after reading the label more closely I found it had little to no sodium. Moreover, unlike on my first successful ride across the state, this time I had not been taking electrolyte tabs. This combination, coupled with a copious intake of water during the storm, made for a disastrous result.

Now I knew why my body felt as if it were shutting down during my recent attempts across the state. I had felt so confident in my training preparation that I neglected to ensure proper nutrition. Because I was not consuming enough electrolytes, sweat and urination rates and sodium loss were high early in my ride. As my exertion and sodium loss continued, my blood pressure fell. Since sodium is key for the absorption of food and water from the digestive tract, I stopped absorbing what I was eating and drinking. Nausea and delirium resulted. Even the sight of food and water made me want to retch. This was my body's way of saying it couldn't process anything. When I drank, the water was not absorbed well and sloshed around in my stomach. I could hear the sloshing. What was absorbed could not be retained and was simply urinated out.

I had intended to purchase electrolyte tabs the day before I left for my ride but had been too busy to do so—a nearly fatal blunder.

Just a couple of weeks after I arrived home from the hospital, Bridget and I were able to take a cruise we had planned to celebrate our tenth wedding anniversary. It all seemed unreal, gazing upon the endless expanse of white-speckled blue from our ten-story deck, hurtling through the sea at thirty knots aboard one of the biggest cruise ships in the world. The immense gratitude I had felt after Bridget overcame cancer returned ten-fold as we enjoyed excursions on Nassau, St. Thomas, and St. Maarten.

I struggled with the reversal of our roles—Bridget becoming the caregiver, and me, now, as the recovering patient. I felt bad because my incident was my own fault, and now others, especially Bridget, had to care for me. The naysayers had cautioned me about the risks and "craziness" associated with my venture, but I had failed only because of my own absentmindedness about properly refueling my body. It was a frustrating reality, a senseless mistake, but I would learn from it. I would use it as an opportunity to harden my resolve in aspiring to the "magis." *What more could I do for the greater glory of God?* I did not know what the future held or whether it included more bold adventure, but soon I would be seeking a new challenge. The same sense of restlessness that I had experienced before I met Bridget persisted. I still wanted to do the ride, and I knew I could, but I was also fine with keeping it in the past. I felt lucky just to be alive. Moreover, any far-flung ambitions were tempered by the awesome yet frightening weight of responsibility of parenthood that I felt like never before. My near-death experience reminded me of the fragility of life and the need for me to be around for Jack and Andrew.

In St. Thomas, we took an afternoon excursion on a motorboat to St. John, the site of our honeymoon. Just four miles to the east, the small Caribbean island embodied tropical beauty with brilliant blue-green water, white sand, and verdant hills, and it boasted an even slower, more laid-back pace than California's San Luis Obispo. St. John featured some of the world's most picturesque, pristine beaches, and its diverse marine life was ideal for snorkeling and scuba diving. The island, mostly owned by the U.S. National Park Service, maintained much of its primitive nature with minimal human development. Most of it was uninhabited, and livestock nonchalantly crossed the narrow, winding roads that hugged the shores and ascended steep heights that were densely packed with trees and plant life.

We took a cab to Trunk Bay, and I rented a snorkel and some flippers. The beach was crowded—at least by St. John standards—with a few dozen people. Several were in the water snorkeling along a set of buoys that marked a line of reef stretching several hundred yards into the sea, as others lay on the beach and waded in the shallow water, the waves gently slapping the shore.

I put on my mask and flippers and set out for the buoys. The serene setting of the beach transformed to a meditative silence underwater, the only sound that of my breathing through the snorkel. Yellow and blue and orange fish beamed with a fluorescent radiance and darted to and fro, as the reef life lazily swayed to the beat of the tide. The sun felt good on my back when it reemerged from small clusters of slow-moving clouds. I glided through the water over the entire course of buoys, occasionally diving below for a better view of the vibrant reef life.

When I returned, Bridget was lying on the beach reading a book. I dried off and sat next to her and we began to talk, when a butterfly landed on my shoulder. We looked at it in awe and amazement as it strutted around and stretched its wings before flying away. We said "unbelievable" simultaneously and chuckled.

"It must be a blessing from God," I said, remembering my mom's friend Sue and her love of butterflies.

Bridget agreed.

"Just think, this is where it all began," she said, reflecting on our honeymoon.

I marveled at all we had been through together—"in sickness and in health"—with gratitude and relief, and I looked forward to our future, regardless of what it held, for we were stronger now, emboldened by our faith and trusting more in God because He had provided us the inspiration, motivation, and power to accept our own hardship as a pathway to peace. We had, indeed, been blessed by what I once considered a "momentary inconvenience."

As my gaze fixed upon the water I thought of Bridget's cancer, and it all came back like a geyser bursting in my mind. My hair stood on end and I could feel a tear welling in my eye as I recalled her enduring spirit and everybody who supported and guided us along the way—our family, friends, colleagues, neighbors, the Jesuits, Isaac, Bridget's nurse and entire medical team, our retreat brothers and sisters, and many others. The world of worry melted into an unfathomable, irradiant spectrum of love and possibility and hope, and I felt the warm embrace of the Holy Spirit, knowing that one day, peering upon the ceaseless brink of eternity, everything would be timeless and peaceful and perfect.

"Yep," I replied. "And this is where it all begins."

A school of dolphins surfaced nearby, one by one bobbing up and down in graceful, synchronous unison, their fins perfect and glistening in the choppy water that glittered and sparkled in the sun.

# EPILOGUE

# FIRST PITCH

\* \* \*

C lad in her bright pink Komen Race for the Cure survivor shirt, Bridget stepped onto the newly chalked dirt and manicured grass. More than forty thousand were in attendance at Busch Stadium for the Cardinals game on Mother's Day. The cityscape, capped by the Gateway Arch, emerged from beyond the outfield, and the blue sky was dusted by intersecting vapor trails, the sun beating down with a gentle radiance. It was a crisp, refreshing seventy degrees.

"Throwing out the first pitch is Bridget DuMont, a five-year breast cancer survivor," said the announcer over the PA.

Komen was teaming up with the wives of the Cardinals for their annual Cardinals Wives Breast Cancer Awareness Day. The stands, typically a sea of solid red, were now complemented by thousands of pink-shirted fans. The game coincided with Bridget's five-year anniversary as a survivor. It was a huge milestone. Statistically, the odds of her getting cancer again were now the same as those of someone without any history of the disease.

The announcer continued to describe how Bridget was the top individual fundraiser for the Komen Race for the Cure event. Approaching the mound, she appeared on the gigantic stadium screen, smiling and cheerful. Inside, however, she was timid and nervous, I knew. Bridget was not easily frazzled, but she anticipated this day with great anxiety. She had practiced her pitch several times with the boys and me in the backyard, though her confidence waned when some of her pitches did not make it far enough. "You'll do fine," I had told her. "It's not about the pitch anyway. It's about the fact that you're the one out there." My consolation helped only so much.

Jack, Andrew, and I watched from behind home plate with Komen representatives and some of the Cardinal wives. Andrew wore his Jon Jay jersey. Coincidentally, Jay's wife was there. We had met Nikki at the pre-event luncheon, and Andrew told her Jon was his favorite player. She was surprised and excited. "I've only seen a few fans wear his jersey," she said. "I can't wait to tell Jon about his big fan." On Andrew's baseball team were the sons of three Cardinals. One of them was the son of Jim Edmonds, an eight-time Gold Glover who wore #15 during his career. When Edmonds' son had joined the team, the coach politely asked Andrew if the young prodigy could wear #15. Andrew, who did not know about Edmonds and his storied past, not only told him no, but also added he was wearing #15 for his favorite Cardinal Jon Jay. We told Nikki that story, and she burst into laughter.

The boys had been looking forward to the game since Bridget's invitation from Komen. In their estimation, she had reached celebrity status by getting to throw out the first pitch. Jack, wearing his Matt Holliday jersey, held the video camera and gave his own personal commentary. Bridget and I referred to him as Jack Buck, the famous Cardinals broadcaster. He was immensely knowledgeable about baseball and enjoyed keeping the score of games on a scorecard with his best friend Charlie. They would watch games like two old men, conversing about plays, players, and tactics with seasoned insight. Jack's professional analysis of his mom's ability to throw the ball to home plate was a bit iffy, but he was her biggest cheerleader.

"Come on, Mom," Jack called out. "You can do it. I know you can."

When Bridget reached the mound, she immediately turned around, and with less than a second to situate herself and prepare for the pitch, she reared back and hurled the ball with the motion of a shot putter. The ball veered to the left and bounced a couple of times, and the catcher, played by rookie infielder Matt Carpenter, got up to field the ball. The two met and shook hands.

"I'll bet you've never seen a throw that bad," Bridget said to him.

"I've seen worse," he said, smiling.

Carpenter signed the ball, and they posed for a picture.

Friends and family were in the stands texting us about the throw. One friend said her curveball was better than Orel Hershiser's.

"Life threw us a curveball," I told Bridget. "You just threw it back."

When we got to our seats, we were surprised to see that Bridget's best survivor friend, Jodi, was with her family in the row directly in front of us, an incredible coincidence considering the crowd size. Shortly after she was diagnosed, Bridget had met Jodi through her friend Lori. The two together endured the passing of their dear mutual friend, an experience that deeply affected them and strengthened their friendship. But they were more than just survivors and friends. They were both young mothers who did not settle for simply overcoming cancer. They made a conscious decision to let their experiences change them for the better.

Bridget and Jodi hugged, giddy with excitement. As they talked with such love and respect for one another, like two war veterans reuniting, I thought about a movie we had watched together as a family a few weeks earlier. *The Rookie* was about a thirty-nine-year-old high school baseball coach in Texas, played by Dennis Quaid, who follows his dream to try out for the major leagues. Armed with grit, determination, and a fiery fastball, he eventually earns a starting spot on the Rays. During one particularly poignant scene, he tells his wife, who is skeptical about his ambition, "If you ain't got dreams, you ain't got nothing." It was a powerful moment, and I thought about how Bridget had inspired us all to dream. When the odds were stacked against her and the prospect of death haunted her, she not only prevailed, but she did so with an emboldened faith that would guide and inspire her for the rest of her life. I would forever be grateful for our love that had become richer over time and the positive example she set for our boys.

Jack and Andrew chatted about the game and their choices for the upcoming All-Star contest like experienced broadcasters. An older couple sitting two rows in front of us turned around and smiled and chuckled.

"Those boys have a future in broadcasting," the man said.

The boys' discussion periodically shifted from baseball to ice cream. It was our routine to go to Ted Drewes, a St. Louis landmark known for its frozen custard, following most Cardinals games.

"When are we going to Ted Drewes?" Jack asked.

"Let's go now," I joked, as it was only the third inning.

Bridget chuckled.

"I never thought I would live to see this day," she said, smiling, referring to her milestone as a cancer survivor.

Five years after Bridget was diagnosed with aggressive breast cancer, we celebrated what she had once thought impossible. For most in the stands, it was just another Cardinals game. For us, it was victory. We sat together as a family, all four of us, more united with one another and more grateful to God.

While I had made a full physical recovery and could have returned to cycling, I chose not to. Instead, I decided to spend with Bridget and the boys all the hours I used to spend training. I had learned the cost and sacrifice that came with pushing my limits of endurance, but I knew I would always have an innate drive to do something bigger, or go farther. I had already been contemplating canoeing from St. Louis to the Hudson Bay in northwestern Canada. A few canoeists had made the trip from Minnesota, but never from St. Louis, as far as I knew. The first several hundred miles would be upstream against the mighty Mississippi.

"So when are we paddling to the Hudson Bay?" I asked.

Bridget glanced over, grinned, and rolled her eyes.

"How would you really do that?" Jack responded. "Is that really possible? I'm not so sure."

The little guy chimed in, saying, "I'll go."

Bridget resumed talking with Jodi. She told her how she was planning to register Bridget's Brigade as an official charity, with much of the funds benefiting breast cancer research and the rest going to local families struggling with cancer. They discussed uniting their fundraising efforts for the next Komentucky Derby, with Jodi hosting a derby party in her hometown in Illinois before expanding to other cities. As they traded ideas with one another, Bridget seemed to glow with life, speaking with energy, enthusiasm, and excitement. Her smile and radiance reminded me of everything good that had come into my life, all the love and hope, an unending gratitude to God, and our two greatest gifts, Thunderbird and Sharp Arrow.

29002608R00129

Made in the USA
Charleston, SC
28 April 2014